MARKET LEADER

Course Book

PRE-INTERMEDIATE
BUSINESS ENGLISH

David Cotton David Falvey Simon Kent

Longman

FINANCIAL TIMES
World business newspaper.

Map of the book

	Discussion	Texts	Language work	Skills	Case study
Unit 1 **Careers** page 6	Discuss ideas about careers	Reading: Response to an advertisement for women tube drivers – *Daily Telegraph* Listening: An interview with the head of a public relations company	Words that go with *career* Modals 1: ability, requests and offers	Telephoning: making contact	Fast-Track Inc.: Choose the best candidate for the job of sales manager Writing: memo
Unit 2 **Selling online** page 14	Discuss shopping online	Reading: Virtual pocket money – *Financial Times* Listening: An interview with the developer of an online bookshop	Words and expressions for talking about buying and selling Modals 2: *must, need to, have to, should*	Negotiating: reaching agreement	Lifetime Holidays: Negotiate a joint venture Writing: e-mail
Unit 3 **Companies** page 22	Discuss types of companies	Reading: A website for a clothing company Listening: An interview with the sales manager of a motorcycle manufacturer	Words for talking about companies Present simple and present continuous	Presenting your company	Valentino Chocolates: Prepare an investment plan Writing: memo
Revision unit A page 30					
Unit 4 **Great ideas** page 34	Discuss ideas	Reading: Three articles about great ideas Listening: An interview with a managing director	Verb and noun combinations Past simple and past continuous	Successful meetings	Fabtek: Choose the best ideas for three new products Writing: memo report
Unit 5 **Stress** page 42	Discuss causes of stress Discuss gender-related qualities Discuss and rank stressful jobs	Reading: A career change – *The Times* Listening: An interview with an authority on stress management	Words about stress in the workplace Past simple and present perfect	Participating in discussions	Genova Vending Machines: Develop a plan to reduce stress Writing: memo
Unit 6 **Entertaining** page 50	Discuss corporate entertaining	Reading: Corporate entertaining in Japan – *Financial Times* Listening: An interview with an expert on corporate entertaining	Words for talking about eating and drinking Multi-word verbs	Socialising: greetings and small talk	Organising a conference: Choose the best location Writing: e-mail
Revision unit B page 58					

Grammar reference: page 118 **Writing file:** page 130

Activity file: page 136   **Audio scripts**: page 143   **Glossary of business terms**: page 153

Introduction

What is Market Leader and who is it for?

Market Leader is a pre-intermediate level business English course for businesspeople and students of business English. It has been developed in association with the *Financial Times*, one of the leading sources of business information in the world. It consists of 12 units based on topics of great interest to everyone involved in international business.

If you are in business, the course will greatly improve your ability to communicate in English in a wide range of business situations. If you are a student of business, the course will develop the communication skills you need to succeed in business and will enlarge your knowledge of the business world. Everybody studying this course will become more fluent and confident in using the language of business and should increase their career prospects.

The authors

David Falvey *(left)* has over 20 years' teaching and managerial experience in the UK, Japan and Hong Kong. He has also worked as a teacher trainer at the British Council in Tokyo, and is now Head of the English Language Centre and a Principal Lecturer at London Guildhall University.

Simon Kent *(centre)* has 15 years' teaching experience, including three years as an in-company trainer in Berlin at the time of German reunification. He is currently a Lecturer in business and general English, as well as having special responsibility for designing new courses at London Guildhall University.

David Cotton *(right)* has over 30 years' experience teaching and training in EFL, ESP and English for Business and is the author of numerous business English titles, including *Agenda, World of Business, International Business Topics*, and *Keys to Management*. He is also one of the authors of the best-selling *Business Class*. He is currently a Senior Lecturer at London Guildhall University.

What is in the units?

Starting up
You are offered a variety of interesting activities in which you discuss the topic of the unit and exchange ideas about it.

Vocabulary
You will learn important new words and phrases which you can use when you carry out the tasks in the unit. A good business dictionary, such as the *Longman Business English Dictionary,* will also help you to increase your business vocabulary.

Discussion
You will build up your confidence in using English and will improve your fluency through interesting discussion activities.

Reading
You will read authentic articles on a variety of topics from the *Financial Times* and other newspapers and books on business. You will develop your reading skills and learn essential business vocabulary. You will also be able to discuss the ideas and issues in the articles.

Listening
You will hear authentic interviews with businesspeople. You will develop listening skills such as listening for information and note-taking.

Language review
This section focusses on common problem areas at pre-intermediate level. You will become more accurate in your use of language. Each unit contains a Language review box which provides a review of key grammar items.

Skills
You will develop essential business communication skills such as making presentations, taking part in meetings, negotiating, telephoning, and using English in social situations. Each Skills section contains a Useful language box which provides you with the language you need to carry out the realistic business tasks in the book.

Case study
The Case studies are linked to the business topics of each unit. They are based on realistic business problems or situations and allow you to use the language and communication skills you have developed while working through the unit. They give you the opportunities to practise your speaking skills in realistic business situations. Each Case study ends with a writing task. A full writing syllabus is provided in the Market Leader Practice File.

Revision units
Market Leader Pre-Intermediate also contains four revision units, based on material covered in the preceding three Course Book units. Each revision unit is designed so that it can be done in one go or on a unit-by-unit basis.

Careers

❛Choose a job you love and you will never have to work a day in your life.❜

Confucius (551–479 BC), Chinese philosopher

Starting up

A **Discuss these questions.**

1 Are you ambitious? Why or why not?

2 Do you have a career plan? Where do you want to be in 10 years' time?

3 Which of the following would you prefer to do?
   a) Work for one company during your career
   b) Work for several different companies
   c) Work for yourself

B **Which of the following areas do you work in (or would you like to work in)? Why?**

1 Sales and marketing

2 Finance

3 Management

4 Administration and personnel

5 Production

6 Research and development (R&D)

C **What should you do to get ahead in your career? Choose the four most important tips from the list below. Compare your ideas in a group and try to agree on a final choice.**

1 Change companies often

2 Use charm and sex appeal with your superiors

3 Attend all meetings

4 Go to your company's social functions

5 Be energetic and enthusiastic at all times

6 Be the last to leave work every day

7 Find an experienced person to give you help and advice

8 Study for extra qualifications in your free time

Vocabulary
Career moves

A The phrases below all include the word *career*. Match them to their correct meanings. Use a good dictionary to help you.

1 career ladder   **a)** something you do in order to progress in your job

2 career move   **b)** period of time away from your job to, for example, look after your children

3 career break   **c)** series of levels that lead to better and better jobs

4 career plan

5 career opportunities   **d)** chances to start/improve your career

    e) ideas you have for your future career

B Complete these sentences with the verbs from the box. Use a good dictionary to help you.

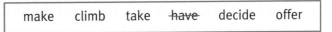

| make | climb | take | ~~have~~ | decide | offer |

1 Employees in large multinationals ......*have*...... excellent career opportunities if they are willing to travel.

2 Some people .... a career break to do something adventurous like sailing round the world or going trekking in India.

3 One way to .... a career move is to join a small but rapidly growing company.

4 In some companies it can take years to .... the career ladder and reach senior management level.

5 Certain companies .... career opportunities to the long-term unemployed or to people without formal qualifications.

6 Ambitious people often .... on a career plan while they are still at school or university.

C Look at the groups of words below. Cross out the noun or noun phrase which doesn't go with the verb in each group.

1 *make*   a fortune
progress
a living
~~a training course~~

2 *get*   progress
a promotion
the sack
a nine-to-five job

3 *earn*   a bonus
a part-time job
money
40 thousand

4 *do*   research
a mistake
a job
your best

5 *take*   a pension
time off
early retirement
a break

6 *work*   flexitime
anti-social hours
overtime
an office job

D Make sentences using the phrases in Exercise C. For example, *You can make a fortune with a career in computers.*

Listening

Human resources and recruitment

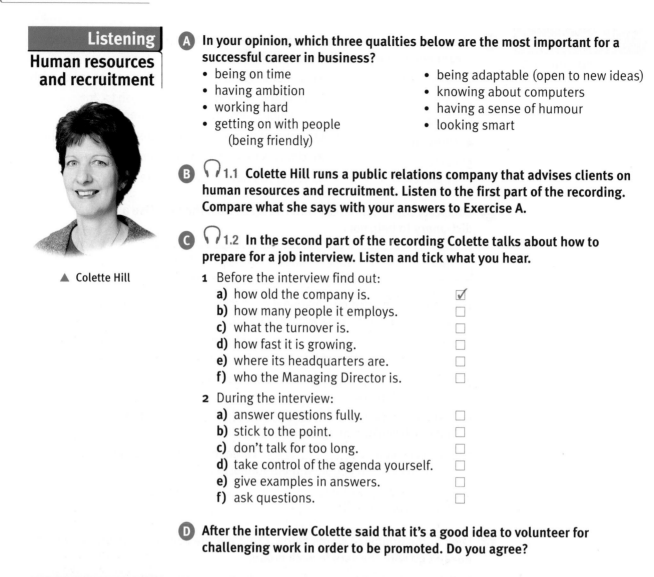

▲ Colette Hill

A In your opinion, which three qualities below are the most important for a successful career in business?

- being on time
- having ambition
- working hard
- getting on with people (being friendly)

- being adaptable (open to new ideas)
- knowing about computers
- having a sense of humour
- looking smart

B 🎧 1.1 Colette Hill runs a public relations company that advises clients on human resources and recruitment. Listen to the first part of the recording. Compare what she says with your answers to Exercise A.

C 🎧 1.2 In the second part of the recording Colette talks about how to prepare for a job interview. Listen and tick what you hear.

1 Before the interview find out:
   a) how old the company is. ☑
   b) how many people it employs. ☐
   c) what the turnover is. ☐
   d) how fast it is growing. ☐
   e) where its headquarters are. ☐
   f) who the Managing Director is. ☐

2 During the interview:
   a) answer questions fully. ☐
   b) stick to the point. ☐
   c) don't talk for too long. ☐
   d) take control of the agenda yourself. ☐
   e) give examples in answers. ☐
   f) ask questions. ☐

D After the interview Colette said that it's a good idea to volunteer for challenging work in order to be promoted. Do you agree?

Reading

Female train drivers

A Are certain careers more suitable for women than for men? Which do you consider a) for women only? b) for men only? c) for either? Include other careers.

- soldier
- police officer
- car mechanic

- nurse
- chef
- pilot

- teacher
- hairdresser
- politician

B Look at the advertisement below from the popular UK women's magazine *Cosmopolitan*. Do you think many people applied? Why or why not?

UNDERGROUND We believe in opening doors for women train operators
£27,656 (after completion of training)

C **Now read the article. What do these numbers in the article refer to?**

a) 1,400   *readers who applied for the job*

b) 4.45

c) 27,650

d) eight

e) one

f) 100

g) three

Cosmopolitan readers queue for Tube job

BY PAUL MARSTON, TRANSPORT CORRESPONDENT

MORE than 1,400 readers of *Cosmopolitan* have applied to become a London Tube train driver. London Underground described the response to its single advert in this month's issue as 'exceptional'.

Successful applicants will have to get out of bed for regular 4.45 a.m. starts, but the £27,650 salary and up to eight weeks' holiday may prove sufficient compensation.

Lorraine Candy, editor of *Cosmo*, said the interest her readers had shown demonstrated that young women were not bound by traditional career patterns.

'It's always been a classic thing for boys to want to be train drivers. Now we're seeing that girls can do it too,' she said.

'I don't think the job is boring or unsexy and I'm sure the passengers couldn't care less whether the train is being driven by a man or a woman – as long as it's on time.'

The ability to break bad news to travellers more sympathetically is one reason London Underground is keen to increase its number of female drivers from 100 – just three percent of driving staff.

From the *Daily Telegraph*

D **Answer these questions about the article.**

1 How many adverts did London Underground put in *Cosmopolitan*?

2 What are the advantages and disadvantages of the job?

3 What do passengers care about most?

4 Why does London Underground want to hire more women?

Language review

Modals 1: ability, requests and offers

Modal verbs are very common in English. Match these functions to the examples: making an offer, describing ability, making a request.

- ....

  Can you help me?
  Could you repeat that, please?

- ....

  Can I help you?
  Would you like a drink?

- ....

  I *can* speak French and Spanish.
  He *could* speak four languages before he was ten.

➡ page 118

A Rearrange the words in 1 to 9 to make questions from a job interview. Then decide whether each question is a) making a request, b) making an offer or c) asking about ability.

1 get you can I anything?
  Can I get you anything? (making an offer)

2 details contact your confirm I could?

3 can you software package use this?

4 speak languages any other you can?

5 about tell you job us your present more could?

6 tell your current salary me you could?

7 would you as soon as possible your decision let us know?

8 start you when can?

9 like coffee some more you would?

B Match the questions in Exercise A with the interviewee's answers below.

a) It's 43 thousand.   6

b) Yes, I use it a lot in my current job.

c) I can let you know next week.

d) Thank you. A coffee, please.

e) Yes, the address is the same, but my e-mail has changed.

f) I'd love some. Thank you.

g) Well, I'm currently responsible for European sales.

h) Yes, I can speak French and Spanish.

i) My notice period is two months.

C Work in pairs. Role play a Sales Director interviewing a candidate for the job of Sales Representative. Make questions with the words below.
For example, *'Can you drive?'*

- drive
- work at weekends
- work on your own
- meet sales targets
- use a computer
- travel frequently
- use spreadsheets
- start next month
- speak any other languages

Skills

Telephoning: making contact

A What kinds of telephone calls do you make in English? What useful telephone expressions do you know?

B 🎧 1.3, 1.4, 1.5 Listen to three phone calls and answer these questions.

1 What is the purpose of each call?   2 Do the callers know each other?

C 🎧 1.3 Listen to the first call again. Complete the expressions on the right so they have the same meaning as the ones on the left.

1 Can I talk to ...?	I'd *like* *to* *speak* *to* ...
2 Just a moment ...	Thank you. ....
3 I'll connect you.	I'll ....
4 Am I speaking to Carmen Diaz?	Hello. .... Carmen Diaz?
5 Yes, it's me.	....
6 The reason I'm calling is ...	Yes, I'm .... your advert ...
7 Can I have your name and address?	.... your name and address?

D 🎧 1.4 Listen to the second call again and complete these phrases.

A Hello. *Could* *I* *speak* [1] to Andrea, please?

B .... [2] she's not here at the moment. Can I .... [3] a .... [4]?

A Yes, please. .... [5] Jacques from Intec. .... [6] you .... [7] her I won't be able to .... [8] the training course on Saturday. She can .... [9] me .... [10] if there's a problem. I'm .... [11] 0191 498 0001.

B OK. Thank you. Bye.

E 🎧 1.5 Listen to the third call again. Underline each phrase the speaker uses.

Dave   Hi, John. Dave here.

John   Oh, hello, Dave. *How are things? / How are you?* [1]

Dave   Fine, thanks. Listen, just a *quick word / quick question.* [2]

John   Yeah, go ahead.

Dave   Do you think you could *give me / let me have* [3] the fax number for Workplace Solutions? I can't get through to them. Their phone's always *busy / engaged.* [4]

John   I've got it *here / right in front of me.* [5] It's 020 7756 4237.

Dave   Sorry, I didn't *hear / catch* [6] the last part. Did you say 4227?

John   No, it's 4237.

Dave   OK. Thanks. Bye.

John   *No problem. / Don't mention it.* [7] Bye.

F Study the Useful language box below. Then role play the telephone calls. Student A, turn to page 136. Student B, turn to page 138.

Useful language

Making calls
Could I speak to Laurie Thompson, please?
Yes, this is Ernesto Badia from KMV.
I'm calling about ...
Could you tell him/her that I rang?
Could you ask him/her to call me back?

Receiving calls
Who's calling, please?
Could you tell me what it's about?
I'll put you through.
Can you hold?
I'm afraid there's no answer. Can I take a message?

Fast-Track Inc.

Background

Fast-Track Inc., based in Boston, US, sells corporate training videos and management training courses. Fast-Track is looking for a new Sales Manager for its subsidiary in Warsaw, Poland. Fast-Track advertised the vacancy only inside the company as it believes in offering career opportunities to its staff.

The subsidiary's recent sales results were poor. Sales revenue was 30% below target. The reasons are:

- Sales representatives are not motivated and staff turnover is high.

- The previous manager had no clear strategy for developing sales in the area.

- Only a few sales contracts were made with client companies' senior managers.

A new appointment

There are three candidates for the position of Sales Manager, Central and Eastern Europe.

They all already work for Fast-Track either in Boston or in Poland. The successful candidate will be based in Warsaw. Here is an extract from the job description for the position.

The successful candidate will be responsible for:

- developing sales, achieving results and increasing customer numbers

- managing the sales team so that it is more motivated, dynamic and effective

He/She will be:

- a natural leader

- energetic, enthusiastic and determined

- confident and outgoing

He/She will have:

- strong sales ability

- organisational and interpersonal skills

- a good academic background and suitable experience

- numeracy skills and the ability to handle administration

- linguistic ability

The position will involve frequent travel throughout the region.

Profiles of the candidates

🎧 **1.6, 1.7, 1.8** Read the essential information about each candidate on page 13. Then listen to the interview extracts.

Joanna Pelc

Polish, aged 30

Education Finished secondary school. Diploma in Marketing.

Experience Has worked for Fast-Track as a sales representative since leaving school. Has a good knowledge of computing.

Achievements Has had the best sales results of the team during the last five years. She looks after some of the company's most important customers.

Languages Excellent Polish and Russian. English – good vocabulary but not very fluent.

Interviewer's comments Very strong personality. Energetic and confident. Sometimes appeared aggressive during the interview. Will she be a good team player?

Robert Kaminsky

Polish, aged 52

Education University degree (Engineering)

Experience Wide experience in a variety of industries. Joined Fast-Track five years ago as Regional Manager for the south of Poland.

Achievements Has been fairly successful, increasing sales by 12% over the five-year period.

Languages Fluent Polish and English.

Interviewer's comments Very calm and relaxed, he moves and talks slowly. A hard worker. He never leaves the office before seven in the evening. Not creative but happy to get ideas from the creative members of a team. Respected by previous staff. Current staff think he is practical and reliable.

Task

1 Work in groups. You are members of the interviewing team. Discuss the strengths and weaknesses of each candidate. Decide who to select for the vacant position. Note down your reasons for your choice.

2 Meet as one group. Discuss your choices. Decide who should fill the vacant position.

Anna Belinski

German, aged 42

Education University degree (History)

Experience Over 15 years as a sales representative in Germany, the US and Poland. Joined Fast-Track a year ago. Has some experience designing websites for companies.

Achievements A good sales record in all her previous jobs. In her first year with Fast-Track her sales results have been satisfactory.

Languages Fluent German, English and Polish.

Interviewer's comments Quiet but knows her own mind. Rather nervous at the interview. Might be good at team building but would probably depend too much on other people. Had some interesting ideas for developing our website. Good at computing and handling figures. Likes administration. Didn't seem to have many ideas about the future of the company.

Writing

Complete this memo from the head of the interviewing team to the Sales Director of Fast-Track.

➡ *Writing file* page 131

Memo

To:	Sales Director
From:	Head, Interviewing team
Subject:	Appointment: Sales Manager, Central and Eastern Europe

We recently interviewed three candidates for this position.

We have decided to appoint ...

I will briefly describe the candidate's strengths and explain the reasons for our decision. ...

Selling online

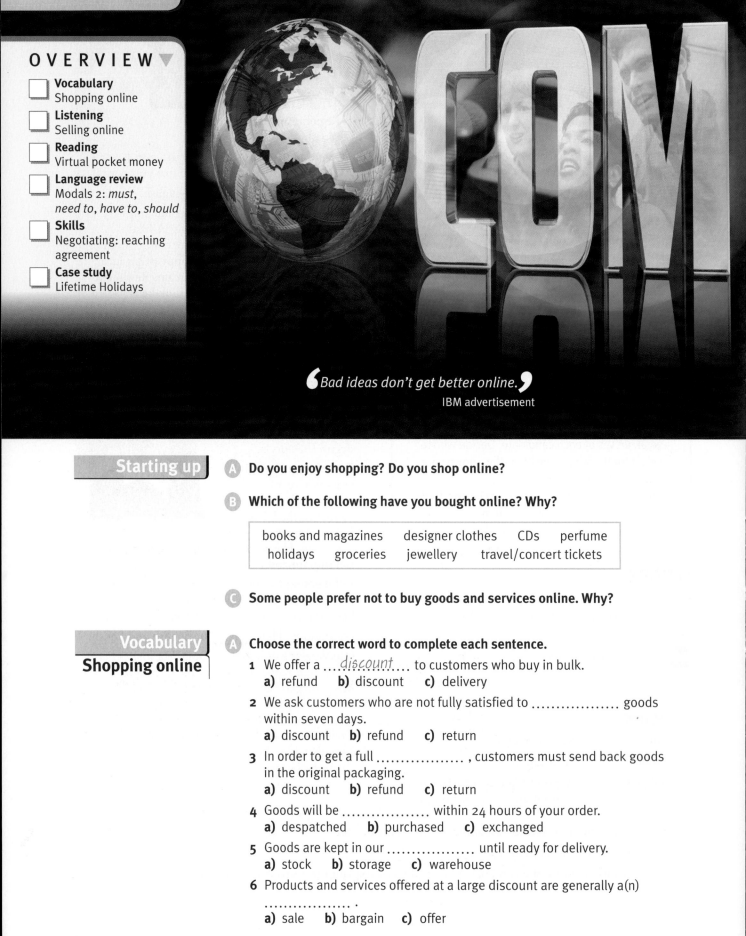

❛*Bad ideas don't get better online.*❜
IBM advertisement

Starting up

Ⓐ **Do you enjoy shopping? Do you shop online?**

Ⓑ **Which of the following have you bought online? Why?**

> books and magazines   designer clothes   CDs   perfume
> holidays   groceries   jewellery   travel/concert tickets

Ⓒ **Some people prefer not to buy goods and services online. Why?**

Vocabulary

Shopping online

Ⓐ **Choose the correct word to complete each sentence.**

1 We offer a ....*discount*.... to customers who buy in bulk.
   a) refund   **b)** discount   **c)** delivery

2 We ask customers who are not fully satisfied to .... goods
   within seven days.
   a) discount   **b)** refund   **c)** return

3 In order to get a full .... , customers must send back goods
   in the original packaging.
   a) discount   **b)** refund   **c)** return

4 Goods will be .... within 24 hours of your order.
   a) despatched   **b)** purchased   **c)** exchanged

5 Goods are kept in our .... until ready for delivery.
   a) stock   **b)** storage   **c)** warehouse

6 Products and services offered at a large discount are generally a(n)
   ....
   a) sale   **b)** bargain   **c)** offer

B Combine words from boxes A and B. Make phrases that match definitions 1 to 7. For example, *credit card details – 2 the name, number and expiry date on your credit card.*

A			
~~credit card~~	cooling off	money back	method of
interest-free	out of	after sales	

B			
guarantee	stock	period	credit
~~details~~	service	payment	

1 the time when you can change your mind and cancel an order

2 the name, number and expiry date on your credit card

3 the way you choose to buy the goods you want

4 when you can pay some time after you buy, but at no extra cost

5 when the goods you require are not available

6 a promise to give your money back if you are not happy

7 the help you get from a company when you start to use their product

Listening

Selling online

▲ Simon Murdoch

A 🎧 2.1 **Simon Murdoch set up the online bookshop Amazon.co.uk. Listen to the first part of the interview and complete the extracts below.**

Before ordering

First, you must have a ....*good*.... ...*website*...[1] and the website needs to be ....[2] and ....[3] to use. It needs to provide ....[4] about the items that you're buying. And the prices on there need to be, you know, ...[5], good prices.

After ordering

And then, once somebody's ordered something from your website, you need to provide a fast ....[6] which is reliable. And then, if anything should go wrong, it's important that you have an excellent ....[7] team dealing with enquiries on the phone or by e-mail.

B 🎧 2.2 **Listen to the second part of the interview. Answer these questions about the online company e-toys.**

1 What was good about e-toys?   2 What problems did e-toys have?

C 🎧 2.3 **Listen to the last part of the interview. Simon describes the main differences between selling online and high street retailing. Which of these statements are true, according to Simon?**

1 Selling online is similar to selling by mail order in many ways.

2 Warehouses are not essential when selling online.

3 Location is more important for online selling than for high street retailing.

4 High street retailers need to present goods attractively to get people to buy.

D **Discuss these questions.**

1 What other differences between online selling and high street retailing can you think of?

2 What are the similarities between the two types of businesses?

Reading

Virtual pocket money

A **Discuss these questions.**

1 What do you think teenagers like to buy online?

2 What problems do you think teenagers have buying online?

B **Look at the article quickly. Compare your answers to Exercise A with what the writer says.**

C **Now read the article more carefully. Which of these statements are true?**

1 Adults spend a greater proportion of their money online than teenagers.

2 Most teenagers pay for goods online with their own credit cards.

3 More than 66% of teenagers in the US and the UK have Internet access.

4 Most teenagers in the US and the UK have bought something online.

5 Children find it easier to persuade parents to buy in a shop than online.

The arrival of virtual pocket money

Financial services companies are rushing to provide teenagers with easier ways of spending their savings online, says **John Willman**

They like using the Internet. They have lots of money to spend. And they spend a higher proportion of it online than the rest of us. Teenagers are just the sort of people an Internet retailer wants to sell to, and the things they want to buy – games, CDs and clothing – are easily sold on the Web.

But paying online is a tricky business for consumers who are too young to own credit cards. Most have to use a parent's card. 'Kids are frustrated with the Web,' says Phil Bettison, European Managing Director of WorldPay, an Internet payments company. 'They want a facility that allows them to spend money.'

That may come sooner than they think: new ways to take pocket money into cyberspace are springing up on both sides of the Atlantic. If successful, these products could provide an important stimulus to online sales.

In general, teenagers spend enormous amounts: Visa calculates it totalled $153bn in the US last year, while the UK market is estimated at £20bn ($29.4bn) annually by NOP, the market research group. Most teenagers have access to the Internet at home or at school – 88 percent in the US, 69 percent in the UK.

One in eight of those with Internet access has bought something online – mainly CDs and music. In the US, 12- to 17-year-olds spend an average of six hours a month online, according to Jupiter Research. One in six buys things over the Internet, with CDs, books, games, videos and clothing the most popular items.

In most cases, parents pay for these purchases with credit cards, an arrangement that is often unsatisfactory for them and their children:

'Pressing parents to spend online is less productive than pressing on the high street. A child who sees a pair of shoes in a shop can usually persuade the parent to buy them. They're more likely to ask "Why?" if you ask to spend some money online,' says Mike Young of Mondex, the electronic payments company.

One way to help them convert notes and coins into cybercash is through prepaid cards such as InternetCash in the US and Smart cards in the UK. Similar to those for pay-as-you-go mobile telephones, they are sold in amounts such as £20 or $50 with a concealed 14-digit number that can be used to load the cash into an online account.

From the *Financial Times*

FINANCIAL TIMES
World business newspaper.

D **What do these words in the article refer to?**

1 *they* (lines 1–22) *teenagers*   4 *these* (line 59)

2 *that* (line 23)   5 *them* (line 62)

3 *that* (line 25)   6 *them* (line 76)

E **Do the following words have a positive or a negative meaning? Write + or – next to each one.**

1 *tricky* (paragraph 2)   4 *unsatisfactory* (paragraph 6)

2 *frustrated* (paragraph 2)   5 *productive* (paragraph 6)

3 *successful* (paragraph 3)

F **Do you agree with this statement? Give your reasons.**
'Teenagers should not have the freedom to buy online.'

page 119

Language review

Modals 2: *must*, *need to*, *have to*, *should*

- We often use *must*, *need to* and *have to* to talk about strong obligation and necessity.
  *Customers **must** be confident that their credit card details are secure.*
  *Online retailers **need to** offer guarantees to their customers.*
  *The site **has to** work quickly and effectively.*

- We can use *should* to give advice.
  *Online retailers **should** acknowledge all orders by e-mail.*
  *Websites **shouldn't** be too complicated.*
  There is no obligation to follow the advice (but it is good practice).

- We use *don't have to* and *don't need to* to talk about lack of obligation.
  *You **don't have to** queue up when you buy online.*
  *If you buy now, you **don't need to** pay anything until next year.*

- We use *mustn't* to talk about prohibition.
  *Advertisers **mustn't** make false claims about their products.*

A **Read these rules of an online book club. Then answer the questions.**

> 📖 You must be 18 or over.
> 📖 You shouldn't give your password to anyone.
> 📖 You don't have to buy every month.
> 📖 You don't have to buy our recommendations.
> 📖 You need to buy ten books per year.
> 📖 You don't have to pay after each purchase.
> 📖 You must pay within three months.

1 Can you join if you are 17?   *No*
2 Can you give your password to a friend if you want to?
3 Is it necessary to buy a book every month?
4 Is it necessary to buy the recommendations?
5 Can you buy only five books per year?
6 Is it necessary to pay after each purchase?
7 Is it necessary to pay within three months?

B **Complete sentences 1 to 8 with suitable endings a) to h).**

1 It's getting late
2 I can work from home
3 I've been transferred to Madrid
4 This deal is too important to lose
5 We lost our database once before
6 I'm afraid this report is urgent
7 I think we're all in agreement
8 We've still got plenty of stock in the warehouse

a) so we don't need to order any more yet.
b) so we must not make a mistake.
c) so you must not forget to back up the files.
d) so you'll have to stay and finish it.
e) so I have to learn some Spanish.
f) so we have to go.
g) so I don't have to go into the office much.
h) so we don't need to discuss it any further.

C **Look at the transcript of the interview with Simon Murdoch on page 144. Then write a list of tips for an online retailer. For example, *Your website must be easy to use.***

Skills

Negotiating: reaching agreement

Ⓐ Work in two groups, A and B. Group A looks at the negotiating tips below. Group B looks at the negotiating tips on page 136.
1 Each group agrees on the five most important negotiating tips on their list.
2 Then form new groups with members from Groups A and B. Agree on a *single* list of the five most important tips from *both* lists.

> **Negotiating tips: Group A**
>
> - Be friendly.
> - Have clear aims.
> - Tell the other side what you want.
> - Listen carefully.
> - Pay attention to the other side's body language.
> - Don't change your plan during the meeting.
> - Never be the first to make an offer.

Ⓑ ⌒ 2.4, 2.5, 2.6 You will hear three parts of a negotiation between Michelle, the manager of a bookstore chain, and a website designer. Listen to each part and complete the chart.

Negotiating point	What Michelle wants	What the designer wants	What they agree
Schedule for setting up the website		Two months	
Payment terms	Fixed amount: $6,000		
Website design			Two covers per page

C 🎧2.4, 2.5 **Listen again to the first two parts of the conversation. After each part, complete the missing words. Then check your answers with a partner.**

Part 1

Michelle   Let's talk about the time for setting up the website. We want it in a month's time. That's the end of July.

Designer   It's a bit early. I was hoping to have two months to do the job. If I finish in one month, ...*will*...... ......*you*...... ......*agree*......[1] to reduce the number of pages?

Michelle   Yes, that's no problem. Just do the best you can. Our ....[2] is to have the website up and running as soon as possible.

Designer   OK then, ...[3].

Part 2

Michelle   Now about payment. You want to charge us $50 an hour. That works out at $400 a day, I believe.

Designer   Yes, that's the ....[4] for the job.

Michelle   Well, ...[5] to pay you a fixed amount for the work. We can ....[6] you $6,000.

Designer   I see. Do you ....[7] ask you why you want to pay that way?

Michelle   Well, you see, that way we can control the cost of the project. If we pay you per hour, the cost could become high. It could get out of control. This way, we know where we stand.

Designer   I see. $6,000. Mmm, that could be all right, I suppose, ...[8] I get some money in advance. ....[9] paying me half when I start the work and half at the end?

Michelle   Yes, I think we could arrange that. OK. I ....[10] that.

D 🎧2.6 **Listen again to the third part of the conversation. Note down all the expressions for *agreeing* and *disagreeing*. Decide whether they express a) strong, b) polite or c) hesitant agreement or disagreement.**

E **Role play this situation.**

A representative of a website maintenance company meets a company manager to negotiate a maintenance contract.

Website representative: turn to page 136.
Company manager: turn to page 138.
Read your role cards. Then do the negotiation.

Useful language

Stating aims
We'd like to have it in a month's time.
We must have delivery by the end of next week.

Making concessions
If I have to finish in one month, I'll need to have an extra designer.
That could be all right – as long as I get some money in advance.

Rejecting suggestions
We'd prefer to pay you a fixed amount.

Bargaining
How about paying me half when I start the work?

Focussing the discussion
Let's talk about the time for setting up the website.

Lifetime Holidays

Background

Lifetime Holidays is a package holiday firm. It has many high street shops and a large catalogue of holidays. However, it is currently facing problems. Fewer people are visiting its shops, and demand for its holidays has fallen. Most of its customers are aged over 50, so it now wants to appeal to a wider range, especially those aged 30 to 50. The solution seems to be to sell holidays online.

As Lifetime has no experience of e-commerce, they want to join with an existing online company, DirectSun. DirectSun is a low-budget holiday website. It offers cheap flights to a small range of destinations and can arrange accommodation, insurance and car hire. It has a good customer base, but it wants a bigger catalogue of holidays to offer.

The two firms have met several times and are now ready to negotiate the details of a possible joint venture.

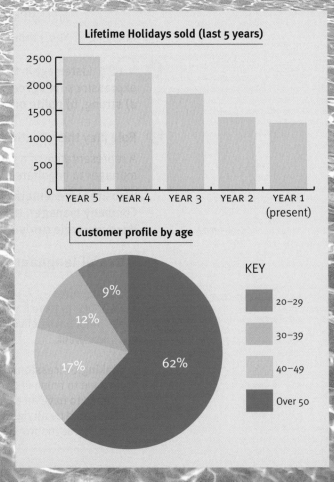

Lifetime Holidays sold (last 5 years)

Customer profile by age

KEY

- 20–29
- 30–39
- 40–49
- Over 50

62%, 17%, 12%, 9%

Task

Work in two groups. You are either
a) a director of Lifetime Holidays (turn to page 138)
b) a director of DirectSun (turn to page 141).
Read your role cards and prepare for the negotiation.
Then, following the agenda below, negotiate each
point. Try to reach an agreement on a joint venture.

AGENDA

1 Length of contract

2 Range of holiday destinations

3 Car hire and insurance

4 Advertising budget

5 Joint venture structure

Writing

As a director of Lifetime Holidays *or* as a director
of DirectSun, complete the e-mail to the person
you negotiated with. Summarise what you
agreed.

Writing file page 133

> **Contract agreement – Message**
>
> Send Save   Insert File... Priority ▾ Options...
>
> This message is being sent with high priority
>
> To...
> Cc...
> Subject: Contract agreement
>
> Arial   10   B I U
>
> Below is a summary of the points we agreed at
> our recent meeting. …

Companies

> ' *Be not afraid of growing slowly; be afraid only of standing still.* '
>
> Chinese proverb

Starting up

A **Which of these companies would you like to work for? Why?**

1 a family owned company

2 a multinational company

3 your own company (be self-employed)

B **Which of these business sectors do you work in (or would you like to work in)? Can you name a company in each sector?**

- Telecommunications / Media
- Engineering
- Retailing
- Construction
- Tourism
- Banking and finance
- Transport
- Vehicle manufacturing
- IT (Information Technology) / Electronics
- Food and drink
- Pharmaceutical
- Other

Vocabulary

Company vocabulary

A **Complete the sentences below with words and phrases from the box.**

> share price   workforce   profit   ~~turnover~~
> subsidiary   market share   head office

1 The amount of money a company receives from sales in a particular period is called its ..... *turnover* ..... .

2 The money a company makes after taking away its costs is its ....

3 A company which is more than 50% owned by a parent company is called a ....

4 The employees in a particular country or business are called the
....

5 The percentage of sales a company has in a particular market is its
....

6 The main building or location of a large organisation is its ....

7 The cost of a company's shares is its ....

B **Complete the extract from a company report with appropriate words or phrases from the box in Exercise A.**

FINANCIAL PERFORMANCE

I am pleased to say the company has continued its excellent performance. We are changing, growing and doing well at a difficult time for the industry. .... *Turnover* ....[1] was €57.2 million, an increase of 15% on last year, and ....[2] rose by 5% to €6.4 million.

We are a highly competitive business. We have increased our ....[3] to 20%. Consequently our ....[4] has risen and is now at an all-time high of €9.6.

Increased production and strong demand have had a positive effect on our cash flow, so we are able to finance a number of new projects. We have successfully moved to our new ....[5] in central London. We are now planning to start full production at the recently opened Spanish ....[6] in October.

Finally, thanks once again to our loyal and dedicated ....[7]. Our employees will always be our most valuable asset.

C **Complete the chart below with the information from the box. Then make sentences about the companies. For example, *Cisco Systems is an American IT company. It supplies Internet equipment.***

> Peugeot   Benetton   container ship operator
> American Express   French   Japanese   Italian
> drug and chemical maker   drinks supplier

Company	Main activity	Nationality
Cisco Systems	Internet equipment supplier	American
	Car manufacturer	
Bacardi Martini		Spanish
	Travel and financial services provider	American
Bayer		German
	Clothing manufacturer	
Sony	Electronic goods maker	
Maersk		Danish

D **Now talk in the same way about your own company or one you know well.**

Listening
Reasons for success

A 🎧 **3.1** Bruno Tagliaferri is UK Sales Manager at Triumph, the British motorcycle manufacturer. Listen to the first part of the interview. What three reasons does he give for Triumph's success?

B 🎧 **3.1** Complete this extract from the first part of the interview.

We've focussed on ....*styling*......¹ and also on the ....² of our product. It's taken a bit of time to build up ....³, but we've done well in the first nine years, and we are now a ....⁴ alternative ....⁵.

C 🎧 **3.2** Listen to the second part of the interview. Which of the following statements are true?

1 The key markets are those in which the most motorcycles are sold.   *true*
2 In France, Triumph has its own subsidiary.
3 Triumph has its own staff in all its overseas markets.
4 Triumph has a poor dealer network which needs to be improved.
5 Buyers of motorcycles are enthusiastic, but they do not know a lot about motorcycles.
6 More than 80% of Triumph's production is sold abroad.
7 France is Triumph's largest market in Europe.

D Discuss these questions.

1 Which brands of motorcycle are most popular in your country?
2 What kinds of people buy motorcycles?
3 Should your government encourage people to use motorcycles in large cities?

Reading
Company website

A What clothing companies do you like? Why do you like them?

B What are the most successful clothing companies in your country?

C Read this text about Zodiac, a highly successful clothing company, and complete the chart. The information is from its company website.

ABOUT ZODIAC INC.

Zodiac Inc. is a global company with three distinct brands – Zodiac, Gemini and Capricorn – and revenues topping $8 billion. The company has its headquarters in Seattle. At the heart of our company are more than 100,000 people worldwide, supporting our catalog and website operations.

Long-term, quality growth has always been a priority at Zodiac Inc. – which is why we're constantly improving the way we sell our products, serve our customers and run our business.

Brands	*Zodiac, Gemini, Capricorn*
Revenues	
Headquarters	
Number of employees	
Main aim	

D Now look at another extract from the Zodiac website. Find the answers to these questions as quickly as you can.

1 In which year did Zodiac:
   a) first sell on the Internet? *1998*
   b) open its first shop abroad?
   c) open its first store for children?
   d) first offer shares?
   e) introduce its own credit card?

2 Where did Zodiac open its first store:
   a) in the US?   **d)** in France?
   b) overseas?   **e)** in Canada?
   c) for babies only?

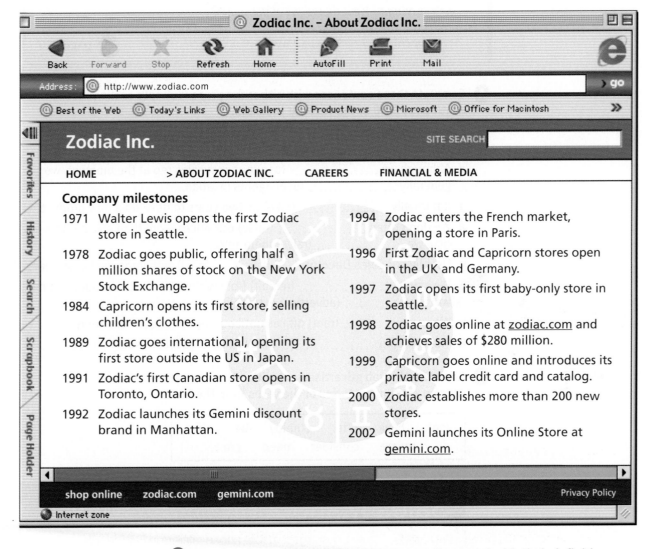

Zodiac Inc. – About Zodiac Inc.

Address: http://www.zodiac.com   › go

Best of the Web   Today's Links   Web Gallery   Product News   Microsoft   Office for Macintosh

Zodiac Inc.

SITE SEARCH

HOME   › ABOUT ZODIAC INC.   CAREERS   FINANCIAL & MEDIA

Company milestones

1971 Walter Lewis opens the first Zodiac store in Seattle.

1978 Zodiac goes public, offering half a million shares of stock on the New York Stock Exchange.

1984 Capricorn opens its first store, selling children's clothes.

1989 Zodiac goes international, opening its first store outside the US in Japan.

1991 Zodiac's first Canadian store opens in Toronto, Ontario.

1992 Zodiac launches its Gemini discount brand in Manhattan.

1994 Zodiac enters the French market, opening a store in Paris.

1996 First Zodiac and Capricorn stores open in the UK and Germany.

1997 Zodiac opens its first baby-only store in Seattle.

1998 Zodiac goes online at zodiac.com and achieves sales of $280 million.

1999 Capricorn goes online and introduces its private label credit card and catalog.

2000 Zodiac establishes more than 200 new stores.

2002 Gemini launches its Online Store at gemini.com.

shop online   zodiac.com   gemini.com   Privacy Policy

Internet zone

E Match words on the left from 'Company milestones' with their definitions.

1 go public   **a)** sell in overseas markets
2 go international   **b)** trade on the Net
3 launch   **c)** offer shares on the stock market
4 go online   **d)** introduce
5 achieve sales   **e)** set up
6 establish   **f)** reach a sales target

F Work in pairs. Tell your partner about a successful company you know. Talk about its products and achievements.

Language review

Present simple and present continuous

Complete the rules with *present simple* or *present continuous*.

We use the .... to:
- give factual information about company activities.
  *Zodiac **has** its headquarters in Seattle.*
- talk about routine activities.
  *I always **check** my e-mail first thing in the morning.*

Some verbs are almost always used in the present simple rather than the present continuous, for example, *like, want, know, need.*

We use the .... to:
- describe ongoing situations and projects.
  *We**'re** constantly **improving** the way we sell our products.*
- describe temporary situations.
  *She**'s staying** in Paris till the end of the month.*
- talk about future arrangements.
  *We**'re opening** a new store next week.*

➡ page 120

A Complete these sentences with either the present simple or the present continuous form of the verbs in brackets.

1 We normally ......*hold*...... (hold) our sales conference in Spain, but this year we ....*held*.. (hold) it in Poland.

2 Although we .... (use) our own sales rep at the moment, we generally .... (use) agents in Japan.

3 It normally .... (take) us two years to develop a new product.

4 We don't often .... (raise) our prices more than 5%, but this time we .... (raise) them 10%.

5 Usually our Sales Director .... (deal) with important customers.

6 We usually .... (recruit) from within the company, but this time we .... (advertise) externally.

7 We .... (rent) offices until our new headquarters are ready.

8 The company .... (want) to achieve record sales this year.

B Complete this job advertisement with either the present simple or the present continuous forms of the verbs from the box.

look	have	offer	employ	be	offer
prepare	consider	need	grow		

Sales Manager Sales Manager

We ...*are*...[1] one of the largest mobile phone retailers in Europe. We ....[2] independent and impartial advice on mobile phones. We ....[3] more than 800 stores in 10 countries, and we ....[4] fast.
We ....[5] over 3,000 workers. Currently we ....[6] the next stage in our development, and we ....[7] for major growth outside Europe.

We ....[8] for people who are reliable, confident and enthusiastic. We ....[9] experienced people who want to work for an expanding company. We ....[10] a competitive salary and private health insurance. We are willing to reward staff with attractive performance-based bonuses.

Ring 020 7946 0008 for an information pack. Ring 020 7946 0008 for an information pack.

Skills

Presenting your company

A **Which of these suggestions do you agree with?**

To make an effective presentation, you should:

1 find out as much as possible about your audience.

2 introduce yourself (name, position, company).

3 start with a joke.

4 outline the structure of your talk.

5 vary the tone of your voice.

6 refer to your notes as often as possible.

7 use clear visual aids.

8 summarise your main points.

B 3.3 **Listen to a presentation about Tara Fashions. Complete the chart.**

Tara Fashions	
Where is the head office?	*Córdoba, Spain*
What does it sell?	
Who are its customers?	
Annual turnover?	
Annual net profits?	
Number of stores: in Spain? in other European cities?	
Strengths?	
Future plans?	

C 3.3 **Listen again. Tick the phrases that you hear in the Useful language box.**

D **Invent a company. Use the headings in Exercise B to help you prepare a presentation about it. Then work in pairs. Make a presentation about the company. Ask questions after your partner's presentation.**

Useful language

Outlining the presentation
First, I'll give you some basic information.
Secondly, I'll talk about our stores in other countries.
Next, I'll talk about career opportunities.
Last of all, I want to look at our future plans.

Introducing new information
Here's some basic information.
Let me add a few figures.
Let's have a look at some statistics.
What are our strengths?

Ending the presentation
To conclude, I want to tell you about our future plans.
Finally, a few words about our new project.
Thanks very much for listening to my talk.
Thanks for coming to my presentation.

Valentino Chocolates

Background

Valentino chocolates are made in Turin, Italy. They are recognised as luxury products with a delicious and unique taste. Some of Valentino's finest chocolates are handmade and have won many international awards.

Expansion

The company started by selling raw chocolate to other chocolate manufacturers. These manufacturers then used it to make their own products. Later, Valentino began selling packaged chocolates directly to the public and created the Valentino brand.

The company expanded fast. It now has almost 300 employees, 75 company-owned shops, and a turnover of €90 million. However, in the last two years, sales growth has slowed down and costs have risen. This has caused a fall in profits (see Chart 1).

Chart 1: Summary of the last three years' results

	Last year	Two years ago	Three years ago
Turnover	€90.5m	€87.2m	€62.6m
Pre-tax profits	€6.4m	€8.2m	€8.9m

Reasons for falling profits

- **Prices**
  There is widespread price cutting in the industry.

- **Production**
  Factory machines often break down.

- **Demand**
  Demand for its Classic Bar is falling. Valentino's new products, biscuits and cakes, are not selling well (see Chart 2).

- **Staff morale**
  Sales staff are becoming demotivated.

Chart 2: Valentino's main products (as a % of turnover)

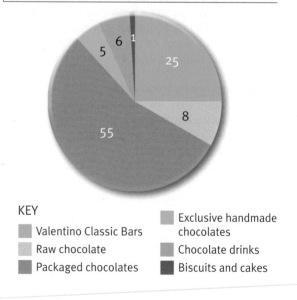

KEY

- Valentino Classic Bars
- Raw chocolate
- Packaged chocolates
- Exclusive handmade chocolates
- Chocolate drinks
- Biscuits and cakes

The future

The company's owners want Valentino to become an international business. They believe it makes the finest chocolates in the world. This year they have set aside €1.5 million to invest in their company. Their problem is to decide how to spend the money so that the company will continue to expand. Recently, a well-known business journal did a profile of the company. It ended as follows:

Valentino can continue to grow, but only if it develops new products and finds new markets.

The ways in which Valentino could invest the €1.5 million are listed in Chart 3.

Chart 3: Investment options

Option	Cost	Benefit
1 Extend the factory	€500,000	Increase the factory's capacity by 30%
2 Buy new machinery	€200,000	End the delays caused by the old machines breaking down
3 Invest in more research and development	€200,000	Develop new products such as a low-fat chocolate drink, new biscuits/cakes
4 Buy out a local competitor	€1.5 million	Reduce local competition
5 Establish a factory in the US	€1.3 million	Manufacture chocolates in a major new market
6 Launch a marketing campaign	€500,000	Increase sales of all products
7 Finance a market survey and research trips to the US	€100,000	Assess the market potential for Valentino products. Contact agents
8 Invest in an existing group of cafés	€500,000	Become a partner in cafés which sell and promote Valentino chocolates
9 Set up online sales	€150,000	Increase sales and profits
10 Buy a new fleet of cars	€500,000	Increase motivation of the sales staff

Task

You are directors of Valentino. Meet to discuss your investment plan.
1 Work in pairs. Decide how to spend the €1.5 million. Prepare a presentation of your investment plan, with reasons for your choices.
2 Meet as one group and present your ideas.
3 As one group, agree on a final investment plan.

Writing

As a director of Valentino Chocolates, write a memo to your CEO outlining your investment plan. Give reasons for your choices. Begin like the example.

 Writing file page 131

Memo

To: CEO
From:
Subject: Investment Plan

In recent years Valentino has become one of Europe's leading brands of chocolate. It is now ready to become a successful international business. The Board of Directors has agreed the following investment plan: ...

Revision

1 Careers

Modals

A Which of these sentences
a) make a request,
b) make an offer,
c) talk about ability?

1 He can type 100 words per minute. *c*
2 Would you like a hand with those bags?
3 She could sell more than all the other salespeople put together.
4 He could program computers in Basic when he was four.
5 Could you help me to write this e-mail – my Spanish isn't very good.
6 Can I get you something to drink?
7 I can dance the samba, but not the tango.
8 May I ask a question?
9 Please would you stop talking – I'm trying to concentrate.
10 They can organise the campaign very quickly.

Reading

B **Turn to the case study on page 12. Look at the information about the job of Sales Manager at Fast-Track. Read a) the requirements in the job description and b) the profile of the first candidate, Joanna Pelc.**

Correct this application letter from the first candidate, Joanna Pelc. In most of the lines 1 to 5 there is one extra word that does not fit. One or two of the lines, however, are correct. If a line is correct, put a tick in the space next to that line. If there is an extra word in the line, write that word in the space.

ul. Nowogrodzka 29
01-215 Warsaw
Poland

Fast-Track Inc.
1225 Federal Street
Boston, MA 02110
USA

25 February 200—

Dear Sir or Madam
I would like to apply for the job of Sales Manager for the
Central and Eastern Europe area. I have worked at Fast-Track
1 since I left school 12 years of ago. I have had some of   1 ....
2 the best results in the sales team, with good knowledge   2 ....
3 of practical sales techniques. However, I also too have   3 ....
4 a Diploma in Marketing, which I obtained by doing   4 ....
5 evening classes at the University of in Warsaw   5 ....
Business School. I believe this combination of
practical experience and qualifications makes me an
ideal candidate for the job that Fast-Track is now
offering.

I am also developing my language skills. I learnt
Russian at school. My English is quite good, and I am
taking evening classes at the University Language
Centre to improve my level.
Of course, I'll be glad to say more about my
suitability for the job if invited for an interview.

Yours faithfully

Joanna Pelc

Joanna Pelc

Writing

Now look at the information for Robert Kaminsky and Anna Belinski on page 13. Write an application letter (not more than 100 words) from one of these candidates based on this information.

2 Selling online

Vocabulary

Complete the crossword.

Across

3 If you don't like it, you can
.... it and we'll give you
your money back. (6)

6 One of the problems of online sales:
.... when the customer is
not at home (8)

7 A building for storing goods (9)

8 Another word for *buy*, or something
that's bought (8)

11 A price reduction often expressed as
a percentage of the original price (8)

Down

1 We must .... our customers
the best products and services. (5)

2 A buyer buys and a seller
.... (5)

4 If you don't like it, you can
.... it for something else of
the same value. (8)

5 Something you think is cheap in
relation to its real value (7)

6 When you send the goods, you ship or
.... them. (8)

9 Money given back to a customer who
has returned goods (6)

10 We don't have any at the moment.
We're out of .... (5)

Modals

In each of these pieces of advice to a traditional high street retailer, find which one of the alternatives is logically *not* possible.

1 Location is the most important thing. You ....*c*....... find a place that lots of people pass every day.
  a) must   **b)** need to   **c)** don't have to

2 Marketing is not as important for high street retailers as for online retailers, and you
.... spend less on advertising than online retailers.
  a) mustn't   **b)** should   **c)** need to

3 You can have a website with a few pages of basic information about your shops, but it .... be very complicated.
  a) should   **b)** needn't   **c)** doesn't have to

4 Great ideas

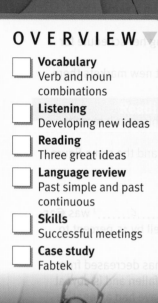

OVERVIEW ▼

❝ *The best way to have a good idea is to have a lot of ideas.* ❞

Dr Linus Pauling (1901–1994), American chemist

Starting up

A **Which of the following statements do you agree with? Which do you disagree with? Why?**

1 There are no *new* ideas.

2 Most of the best ideas are discovered by accident.

3 Research and development is the key to great business ideas.

4 There is nothing wrong with copying and improving the ideas of others.

5 The best way to kill an idea is to take it to a meeting.

B **What should companies do to encourage new ideas?**

Vocabulary
Verb and noun combinations

A **Match the verbs and nouns below to make word partnerships about the benefits companies get from great ideas.**

Verbs		
1 exploit *b)*	3 win	5 enter
2 extend	4 make	6 see
Nouns		
a) an award	c) a range	e) an opening
b) ~~an opportunity~~	d) a market	f) a breakthrough

B Match the verbs and nouns below to make word partnerships about the benefits customers get from great ideas.

Verbs			
1 save *f)*	**3** meet	**5** protect	**7** reduce
2 fill	**4** solve	**6** enhance	
Nouns			
a) waste	**c)** a gap	**e)** a need	**g)** the environment
b) status	**d)** a problem	**f)** time	

C Complete the extract from a talk by the head of a Research and Development Department with the correct form of words from Exercises A and B.

Great ideas are generated in different ways. Sometimes an idea may simply be when a company ....*exploits*.... [1] an opportunity to .... [2] the product range, to offer more choice to existing customers. Or a great idea could allow a company to .... [3] a market which was closed to it before.

Companies which are prepared to spend a lot on R&D may .... [4] a breakthrough by having an original idea for a product which others later copy, for example Sony and the Walkman.

On the other hand, some products are developed in response to customer research. They come from customer ideas. These products .... [5] a real need. Or the product does something similar to another product, but faster, so it .... [6] time. Some people will buy new products because the product .... [7] their status – makes them feel more important. Other people will buy any 'green' product which .... [8] waste or .... [9] the environment, even if it is more expensive.

If an idea is really good – perhaps the product .... [10] a gap in the market – it may even .... [11] an award for innovation.

D 🎧 **4.1** Now listen and check your answers.

Listening

Developing new ideas

▲ Tim Cook

A 🎧 **4.2** Dr Tim Cook is Managing Director at Isis Innovation, which is owned by Oxford University. Listen to the first part of the interview and answer these questions.

1 Isis helps people to make money from new ideas.
  a) Where do the ideas come from?
  b) How does Isis turn them into commercial opportunities?

2 Which of the following companies has Isis started? A company which:
  a) uses technology developed in the university's Engineering Department to make cars go faster.
  b) makes houses for bees in order to grow fruit more efficiently.
  c) sells computers to archaeologists.

B 🎧 **4.3** Listen to the second part of the interview and complete the extract.

To build a company on university ....*science*.... [1], you have to bring together a number of components. The first thing you need is a .... [2], which we help the researchers to .... [3]. We can then use this business plan to raise the .... [4] – the cash that you need to .... [5] the business. This comes from private .... [6] ...

Reading

Three great ideas

A Work in groups of three. Student A reads article 1; Student B reads article 2; Student C reads article 3.

B Complete the parts of the chart which relate to your article.

	Herta Herzog	Richard Sears	Vodafone
Job/Industry	Advertising		
Where idea was created		the US	
Date of idea			1997
Great idea(s)			
Result of idea			

C Exchange information and complete all the sections of the chart.

D When they had their great ideas, what were the following doing?
- Herta Herzog
- Richard Sears
- Vodafone

Article 1

Double your money

IN THE 1970s Herta Herzog, an Austrian psychologist, was working for the Jack Tinker advertising agency in New York. One of their clients was
5 Alka-Seltzer, which manufactured a product for acid indigestion, sour stomach and headaches. At that time the advertising for the product showed a hand dropping one of the tablets
10 into a glass of water. Herzog made a suggestion. She said that the hand in the photograph should drop two tablets into the glass. The advertising was changed and sales of Alka-Seltzer
15 doubled. After the success of the campaign, other manufacturers began to use similar ideas to boost sales.

Article 2

Buying without shops

IN 1891, WHEN American farmers were complaining about high prices in shops in the countryside, Richard Sears had an idea. Sears was an agent of a railway company and
5 at that time he was selling watches with his partner Alvah Roebuck, a watchmaker. His idea was to use the new national railway system and post office to create a new way of selling: mail order. Sears bought in bulk and
10 so kept prices low. He was also good at attracting customers with advertising. By 1895 the Sears catalogue had 532 pages. The company was expanding fast, so it moved to a huge building in Chicago. Finally the
15 company developed the first automated warehouse. This improved the capacity of the business by 1,000 percent.

Sears Building, Chicago

Article 3

Pay before you talk

BY THE 1990S many people were using mobile phones for both business and pleasure. They had a contract and received a bill for calls they had made in the previous month.
5 Vodafone, a successful UK mobile phone company, was already making good profits when it introduced its new Pay As You Talk service in 1997. This allowed customers to
10 have a phone without a contract and monthly bills. Instead, they have a 'top up' card to extend calling and service credit. The advantage for customers was that they could carefully budget the amount of money spent –
15 very useful for parents who gave phones to their children. Vodafone's great idea was to get people to pay in advance for their calls. Thanks to this, sales increased.

Fabtek

Introduction

Fabtek is a small company based in Hamburg, Germany. It has produced a new type of fabric called Protean, which can be used for a wide variety of products. Protean has many advantages.

- It is light, strong and long-lasting.
- It can be made very thick or so thin that it becomes translucent.
- It can be made in any colour.
- It is extremely flexible and soft to the touch.
- The fabric is made from fibres similar to nylon and polyester. These are coated with metals so that the fabric can conduct electricity.

Fabtek believes that Protean has great sales potential. At present, it is trying to expand sales by licensing other manufacturers to produce interesting new products with Protean.

Fabtek already has a licensing agreement with one firm, which has produced some award-winning products using Protean. Here are three.

1 'Dazzle' – A range of shoes for young women
   Selling points:
   - Light and comfortable – adapt to the shape of a person's foot
   - Their colour can be changed at any time
   - Shiny, smart and very durable
   - Ideal for dancing

2 Protean steering wheel
   Selling points:
   - Better grip for drivers
   - Safer than all other steering wheels
   - Very pleasant to the touch
   - Low production costs

3 Protean watch straps
   Selling points:
   - Waterproof and easy to clean
   - Anyone can wear them – non-allergic
   - More beautiful than other straps
   - Light up in the dark

An opportunity for Gadget Plc

Recently, Fabtek contacted Gadget Plc, a company with over 2,000 products and a worldwide network of sales offices. Gadget has designed and developed many best-selling electronic, household and automobile products. Fabtek has asked Gadget to come up with new ideas for using Protean. Here is an extract from a letter which Fabtek's Chief Executive sent to Gadget's Development Manager.

We are looking for partners to manufacture products using Protean. We want to work with firms that are creative and which can design exciting, innovative products.

We invite you to send us three concepts for new products in the following form:

1   A description of the product
2   Its selling points
3   Ways in which the product is really new
4   Its target consumers and main buyers
5   Price which will attract the most buyers
6   Places where you can sell it
7   An advertising and promotion plan

Task

Work in small groups. You are a member of Gadget's Product Development Department.

1   Hold a meeting to propose ideas for exciting new products which use Protean. Use the points in the letter as a guide. Discuss the advantages and disadvantages of each proposal.
2   Choose the three products which you will propose to Fabtek in order to get a licensing agreement.

Writing

You are a member of Gadget Plc's Product Development Department. The Chief Executive of Fabtek has asked you to write a memo report on *one* of the products you have chosen. Outline the product's key features and say why it presents a commercial opportunity.

Writing file page 131

MEMO

To   CEO, Fabtek
From   New Product Development Team, Gadget Plc
Subject New product development

This report lists the key features of an exciting new product made from Protean. It also looks at its key selling points and examines its commercial potential.
…

It is not work that kills men, it is worry.

Henry Ward Beecher (1813–1887), American preacher and abolitionist

Starting up

Ⓐ **Which of these situations are the most stressful for you?
Can you add any others?**

- going to the dentist
- queuing in the supermarket
- being stuck in a traffic jam
- going to the hairdresser
- finding a place to park
- organising a (dinner) party
- having an interview
- making a speech
- flying

Ⓑ **What do you do to relax? Which of these activities are the most effective for
you and why? In what other ways do you relax?**

playing a sport	reading	eating/drinking	having a bath
walking	gardening	massage	shopping	listening to music
	watching TV	meditating	surfing the Net

C Rank these situations from 1 (most stressful) to 8 (least stressful). Then discuss your choices.

- making a presentation to senior executives
- leading a formal meeting
- telephoning in English
- writing a report with a tight deadline
- negotiating a very valuable contract
- meeting important visitors from abroad for the first time
- asking your boss for a pay rise
- dealing with a customer who has a major complaint

Can you think of any other stressful situations?

Listening

Dealing with stress

▲ Cary L Cooper

A What do you think are the main causes of stress at work?

B 🎧 5.1 Professor Cary Cooper is a well-known authority on stress management. Listen to the first part of the interview and answer these questions.

1 According to Professor Cooper, what are the two major causes of stress at work?
- Firstly, increasing ....
- Secondly, working ....

2 Does Professor Cooper think these are new problems? Do you agree? Explain why or why not.

C 🎧 5.2 Listen to the second part of the interview. Tick the examples of stress which Professor Cooper mentions.

1 long hours ☑
2 too much paperwork ☐
3 not enough breaks during working hours ☐
4 a difficult boss ☐
5 transport problems going to and from work ☐
6 lack of promotion opportunities for women ☐

D 🎧 5.3 Listen to the third part of the interview. Underline the correct answer, according to Professor Cooper.

1 *Men / Women* are more flexible.

2 *Men / Women* cope with pressure better.

3 *Men / Women* have more stress-related illnesses.

E In your opinion, which of the following apply more to men or women. Why?

Men / Women

1 are better time managers.

2 are less worried about deadlines.

3 have more pressure outside work.

4 are less ambitious.

5 worry more about making mistakes.

6 pay more attention to detail.

7 are better at doing many things at the same time.

8 are more likely to become angry when stressed.

Reading

A career change

A **Before you read the article, discuss these questions.**

1 Did you have a 'dream job' when you were a child?

2 What is the rat race? Is it a
   a) game where people bet money on rats that race?
   b) very busy and competitive way of life?
   c) group of criminals driving fast cars?

3 *To swap* means 'to exchange': true or false?

B **Read the article. Then answer the questions that follow it.**

Banker swaps rat race for bus lane

BY SIMON DE BRUXELLES

A BANK manager has given up his £30,000-a-year job with NatWest to realise his childhood ambition of becoming a bus driver.

Despite the £11,000 salary and anti-social hours, John Burgin, 48, has never been happier. 'Banking was a career but in the end it became just a job,' he said. 'Once I knew I was leaving, I used to go outside at lunchtime and watch as the buses drove up and down. The time had come.'

His passion was awakened as a boy growing up in Sheffield, where he collected bus maps and timetables. But Mr Burgin, from Nailsea, near Bristol, went on to spend nearly 30 years working his way up through NatWest.

'The levels of stress are totally different,' he said. 'At the bank, things were very political. I worked hard all day then took work home, and it never really finished. There is stress in driving a bus around Bristol, but it's a different kind and I don't take it home.'

From *The Times*

1 What job does John Burgin do now? What job did he use to do?

2 How much did he earn? How much does he earn now?

3 What did he collect when he was a child?

4 How long did he work in a bank for?

5 'Banking was a career but in the end it became just a job.' What does Burgin mean by this?

6 Why is Burgin's new job less stressful than his old one?

C **Look at the words below. Which go with the job of a) a bank manager or b) a bus driver? Label them a) or b).**

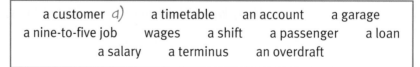

a customer *a)*	a timetable	an account	a garage
a nine-to-five job	wages	a shift	a passenger	a loan
a salary	a terminus	an overdraft

D **Find words and phrases in the article which mean:**

1 to stop doing an activity (paragraph 1).

2 to achieve a dream (paragraph 1).

3 times when people do not usually work, for example the weekend or at night (paragraph 2).

4 to get better and better jobs in the same company (paragraph 3).

5 to do extra work outside the office (paragraph 4).

Vocabulary

Stress in the workplace

A Match the words to their definitions.

1 lifestyle   **a)** a time or date by which you have to do something

2 workaholic   **b)** a system where employees choose the time they start and finish work each day

3 workload

4 deadline   **c)** the way people choose to organise their lives

5 flexitime   **d)** someone who cannot stop working and has no time for anything else

   e) the amount of work a person is expected to do

B Complete each sentence with an appropriate word from the list in Exercise A.

1 I worked until 11 o'clock at night to meet the .... for presenting the report.

2 I work six days a week and never have a holiday. My girlfriend says I'm a ....

3 Karl has a heavy .... at the moment because several colleagues are sick.

4 She gave up a highly paid job to join a meditation group in India. She's completely changed her ....

5 A .... system can help to reduce stress levels of employees by giving them more control over their working hours.

Discussion

Stressful jobs

A Look at the words in the box. Discuss where to put the jobs in the stress league below. Then turn to page 140 and check your answers.

| Actor | Hairdresser | Librarian | Banker | Bus driver | Teacher |

Your place in the stress league

Rating is from ten to zero: the higher the rating, the greater the pressure

Miner	8.3	Musician	6.3	Accountant	4.3
Police officer	7.7	....	6.2	....	4.3
Construction worker	7.5	Social worker	6.0	Solicitor	4.3
Journalist	7.5	Sales assistant	5.7	Architect	4.0
Airline pilot	7.5	Stockbroker	5.5	Optician	4.0
Advertising executive	7.3	....	5.4	Postman	4.0
....	7.2	Psychologist	5.2	....	3.7
Doctor	6.8	Diplomat	4.8	Vicar	3.5
Film producer	6.5	Farmer	4.8	Nursery nurse	3.3
Fireman	6.3	Vet	4.5	....	2.0

Source: University of Manchester Institute of Science and Technology

B Is your own job (or one you intend to do) included in the table? Do you think it is in the right place?
What about the other jobs in the table?
If your job is not included, where would you place it?

C Discuss these questions.

1 Do you like working under pressure? Why or why not?

2 What deadlines do you have to meet in your daily life? Which are the most difficult to meet?

3 Why do people become workaholics?

Language review

Past simple and present perfect

Answer the questions about the sentences in italics.

1 *She has worked in Warsaw for five years.*
  - Does she work in Warsaw now?
2 *She worked in London for three years.*
  - Does she work in London now?

Which sentence (1 or 2) uses the past simple? Which uses the present perfect?

We use the past simple:
- to talk about completed actions that happened in the past.
  *They **worked** over last weekend to meet the deadline.*
- to refer to a definite moment or period in the past.
  *They **made** the presentation on Monday.*

The present perfect connects the past and the present. We use the present perfect:
- to talk about past actions that affect us now.
  *Our company **has** just **introduced** flexitime and everyone's delighted.*
- to talk about life experiences.
  *I've **worked** with many companies where stress was a problem.*
- to announce news.
  *The CEO **has appointed** a new management team.*

→ page 122

A **Cross out the incorrect sentence in each pair.**

1 Stress levels have increased in recent years.
  ~~Stress levels increased in recent years.~~

2 The role of women changed dramatically over the past 100 years.
  The role of women has changed dramatically over the past 100 years.

3 He has worked as a stress counsellor since 1999.
  He worked as a stress counsellor since 1999.

4 I resigned two months ago.
  I have resigned two months ago.

5 Have you ever been to a stress counsellor before?
  Did you ever go to a stress counsellor before?

6 I have seen a stress counsellor last week.
  I saw a stress counsellor last week.

B **Write the time expressions from the box under the correct heading.**

Past simple	Present perfect
two years ago	*so far*

~~so far~~   ~~two years ago~~   ever   in 1999   yet   just
yesterday   for the past two weeks   already   never
last Monday   during the 1990s   over the last few years
since 2001   when I was at university

C **Work in pairs. Ask and answer questions about the subjects below.**

- attend a conference
- be late for an important meeting
- make a telephone call in English
- travel abroad on business
- make a presentation
- go on a training course

A Have you ever attended a conference?   *B Yes, I have.*
A Where was it?   *B In Madrid.*

Skills
Participating in discussions

A 🎧 **5.4** A personnel manager and two colleagues are discussing ways of improving the staff's health and fitness. Listen and note down their suggestions.

B 🎧 **5.4** The speakers use several expressions to make suggestions. Listen again and fill in the missing words.

1 We .... all staff a free medical checkup.

2 .... having a no-smoking policy in the staff restaurant?

3 I think we .... the food.

4 True. We .... the menus and offer healthier meals.

5 .... setting up a counselling service, Vincent?

C 🎧 **5.5** Later in the same meeting they discuss whether to buy group membership to their local Sports Centre. Listen and tick the expressions they use. Then write A if the expression shows agreement, or write D if it shows disagreement.

1 Mm, I don't know.   ✓   D

2 It sounds interesting, but it could be very expensive.   ✓   D

3 I agree with you, Tanya. It'd cost a lot ...

4 I don't agree at all. It's got a very good pool and sauna.

5 Yes, it's worth checking out, I suppose.

6 A sauna is very relaxing, I must admit.

7 Maybe, but there are so many other things we could do.

D Work in pairs. You work in the personnel section of a large bank. Discuss how to deal with the problems below. Use expressions from the Useful language box to help you.

1 Staff often arrive at work late and leave early.

2 Abuse of the telephone and e-mail systems. Staff often use them for personal matters rather than for company business.

3 High staff turnover of front-desk cashiers in all the bank's branches.

Useful language

Making suggestions

We could offer staff a wider choice of food.
Why don't we change the menus?
How about offering healthier meals?
What about having a no-smoking policy?
I think we should send out a questionnaire.
   (strong suggestion)

Giving opinions
I think that we should ask the staff.
I feel that we have to consider the cost.
I'm sure/convinced/positive that people would like it.

Agreeing
Yes, that's right.
I think I agree with you.
Exactly.
Good/Excellent idea.

Disagreeing
Yes, but what about the cost?
I'm not sure I agree.
I really don't agree.
   (strong disagreement)

Genova Vending Machines

Background

Genova Vending Machines (GVM) is part of a multinational company, based in Zurich, Switzerland. GVM merged with another company 18 months ago. As a result of the merger, the management:

- cut the workforce by 15%.

- introduced open-plan offices.

- proposed that salary payments and staff recruitment should be done by outside companies instead of by the Human Resources (HR) Department. If this happens, there will be redundancies in the department.

Most staff are now worried about job security and morale is low. In particular, staff in the Human Resources Department complain of being overworked and severely stressed. Absenteeism is high and several staff have recently resigned.

Consultants' findings

The management has asked a group of consultants to study the problems in the HR Department. They have presented a report of their findings.

Space problems

The HR staff do not like the open-plan office. They don't have enough space or privacy. Many of them work in small areas without windows. The office is noisy and staff are often interrupted by colleagues.

Heavy workloads

Because of the redundancies, staff are working harder and longer hours. Also, they have to attend too many meetings and deal with too much paperwork. The company is monitoring their work more closely and controlling them more than ever before.

Pressure from the redundancy process

Since last year, the HR staff have had to make many colleagues from other departments redundant. Some of the HR staff involved in this have suffered great emotional strain.

Further staff cuts

There is a new rumour about possible further redundancies. The unions have said that they will recommend strike action if this happens.

The new HR Director

The new Director of HR is extremely unpopular. She doesn't listen to people or try to understand their points of view. She often criticises staff and rarely praises them. She never mixes with staff outside office hours.

Career moves

Several good HR personnel say they will resign unless the situation improves.

Task

1 You are members of the group of consultants studying the problems in the HR Department. Work in small groups to discuss these questions.
   - Which problems do you think are the most serious?
   - What should the management do to solve the problems?
2 Meet as one group. Work out an action plan to reduce the stress in the HR Department.

Writing

As leader of the Stress Management Team, write a memo to GVM's Managing Director outlining your recommendations for stress management in the company in both the short and long term.

➡ *Writing file* page 131

Memo

To: **Managing Director, GVM**
From:
Date:
Subject: **Stress Management**

A meeting of the Stress Management Team was held on … . The following recommendations were made:
…

Entitertaining

'There's no such thing as a free lunch.' Anonymous

OVERVIEW ▼

☐ **Listening**
Corporate entertaining

☐ **Vocabulary**
Eating and drinking

☐ **Reading**
Corporate entertaining
in Japan

☐ **Language review**
Multi-word verbs

☐ **Skills**
Socialising: greetings
and small talk

☐ **Case study**
Organising a conference

Starting up

A **Imagine you have to entertain a group of foreign businesspeople. Which of the following activities would you choose? What would you add?**

- historic sites
- bar/nightclub
- theatre
- opera/concerts
- wine tasting
- horse racing
- motor racing
- golf
- football
- tennis
- restaurant
- art galleries

B **Match the six most popular UK events for corporate entertaining to the photographs above.**

1 The Grand Prix
2 Wimbledon
3 The Open Golf Championship
4 The Chelsea Flower Show
5 Royal Ascot
6 Henley Regatta

C **Many companies spend a lot of money on corporate entertaining. Do you think the money is well spent? Why or why not?**

Listening

Corporate entertaining

▲ Tony Barnard

A 🎧 **6.1 Listen to the first part of the interview with Tony Barnard, an expert on corporate entertaining. Then answer these questions.**

1 What kind of entertainment programme do most companies have?
Complete the phrase:
C .... R .... M .... programme.

2 According to Tony, why do companies spend money on corporate entertaining?

3 What other events are mentioned in addition to the 'big six'?

B 🎧 **6.2 Listen to the second part of the interview and answer these questions.**

1 Why is corporate entertaining important for small businesses?

2 What does Tony think about entertaining in times of economic decline?

C **What big events do companies use to entertain customers in your country?**

Eating and drinking

A Put the following into a logical order for entertaining in a restaurant.

a) Look at the menu ☐
b) Ask for the bill (*BrE*) / check (*AmE*) ☐
c) Book a table (*BrE*) / Make a reservation (*AmE*) ☐ *1*
d) Leave a tip ☐
e) Have the main course ☐
f) Have a dessert ☐
g) Order a starter ☐
h) Have an aperitif ☐

B Write the foods below under the correct headings. Add some words of your own.

~~lamb~~	~~broccoli~~	eggs	banana	beef	peas	crab	beans
melon	pasta	lemon	tomato	lobster	fish	potato	cheese
onion	veal	chicken	prawns	apple	mussels	orange	rice

Fruit	Meat	Vegetable	Seafood	Other foods
	lamb	broccoli		

C What are some typical dishes from your country? How would you describe them to a foreign visitor? Use some of the adjectives below and the nouns from Exercise B. Study these examples.

- *It's a kind of seafood/vegetable.*
- *It's a bit like chicken/lamb.*
- *It's quite spicy/rich.*
- *You can eat it with rice/pasta.*

boiled	fried	baked	grilled	roast	steamed	spicy
hot	rich	sweet	salty	delicious	tasty	bland	rare
medium rare	well done

D Match the options in the first box with the drinks in the second box. For example, *black or white coffee*. Add other drinks.

Options

1 black/white *e)*
2 still/sparkling
3 red/white
4 single/double
5 bottled/draught
6 with milk/lemon

Drinks

a) beer
b) wine
c) water
d) tea
e) ~~coffee~~
f) whisky

E Work in pairs. Imagine you are offering a guest a drink. Use words from Exercise D.

Corporate entertaining in Japan

A) How important is corporate entertaining in your:
a) country?   b) industry/organisation?

B) Skim the article below. Then decide which of these headlines is the best.

1   JAPAN SAYS GOODBYE TO KARAOKE NIGHTS

2   JAPAN PREFERS TO SING AS BUDGETS ARE CUT

3   JAPANESE GOVERNMENT TO TAX GIFTS AND ENTERTAINMENT

By Ken Hijino and David Ibison

Hisako Saka, a hostess at a bar called Bouquet in Tokyo's high-class entertainment area, is complaining. 'Customers go home before the last train and order far fewer drinks. They are less cheerful and talk about restructuring all the time,' she said.

'Fewer girls are deciding to become hostesses. My salary has halved.' Corporate entertaining is in steep decline. Newly released figures from Japan's National Taxation Administration have revealed that Japanese companies spent 13.3 per cent less on entertaining and gifts in the year to last January than in the previous year.

The latest figures show spending on entertainment is at its second lowest level since records began in 1961.

The decline indicates that the high spending days of the 1980s are over and that a new phenomenon – cost control – has entered the corporate dictionary.

As the credit environment has tightened, losses have multiplied, restructuring has taken hold and the concept of shareholder value has crossed the Pacific, leading to entertainment budgets being cut. In the boom days some executives would think little of running up a £7,000 bill in one night entertaining an important client.

These days the entertainment still goes on but at more modest establishments. Cheaper restaurants are busier and karaoke parlours are being chosen over expensive nightclubs.

Kunio Sato, a bar owner for the past 35 years in Ginza, Tokyo's most famous

entertainment area, said sadly, 'Companies are much stricter these days with what they will let their employees spend compared with the old days.'

The cost cutting does not end at the bar. Some of Japan's huge conglomerates have cut down ritual corporate gift giving. Budgets for gifts at New Year have, in some cases, been cancelled, forcing employees to buy the gifts themselves, according to an employee at one large conglomerate.

From the outside, the discovery by Japanese companies of basic cost control can be seen as an encouraging development in an economy that had previously let spending run wild.

From the *Financial Times*

FINANCIAL TIMES
World business newspaper.

C) Now read the article carefully. Are the following statements true or false?

1 The number of bar hostesses is increasing.   *false*
2 Spending on entertainment is the lowest since 1961.
3 Saving money is now important to businesses in Japan.
4 Entertaining in restaurants and karaoke bars is still important.
5 Nightclubs are less important for entertaining than in the past.
6 Employees prefer to pay for corporate gift giving themselves at New Year.

D) Find words or phrases in the article which mean:

1 reduced by 50% (paragraph 2)   *halved*
2 decreasing rapidly (paragraph 2)
3 reorganising a company (paragraph 4)
4 a plan of how to spend an amount of money for a period of time (paragraph 4)
5 economically good times (paragraph 4)
6 a large business organisation of several companies (paragraph 7)

E) Compare the situation in Japan with what happens in your own country or company.

Language review
Multi-word verbs

A **multi-word verb** is a verb and one or two particles (prepositions or adverbs). Look at the following examples from the text.
*… executives would think little of **running up** a £7,000 bill …*
*Some of Japan's huge conglomerates have **cut down** ritual corporate gift giving.*

- It may be possible to guess the general meaning of the multi-word verbs above. However, sometimes a new meaning is created.
  *I had to **turn down** their offer of dinner.* (= refuse)
- Some multi-word verbs can be separated from their particles.
  *I **called off** the meeting*, or *I **called** the meeting **off**.* (= cancel)
- Some multi-word verbs cannot be separated.
  *She **paid for** the drinks*, not ~~*She **paid** the drinks **for***~~.

→ page 123

A Match the multi-word verbs in sentences 1 to 8 with their definitions a) to h).

1 Alice is *looking after* some visitors from Taiwan.	a) see the sights
2 They want to *look around* the city before they go.	b) arrive/appear
3 We *look forward to* welcoming their Chief Executive.	c) get involved in
4 Our Sales Manager is *taking* them *out* tonight.	d) give attention to/protect
5 We hope all staff can *take part in* the visitor programme.	e) accept (an offer)
6 We'd like to *take up* your invitation to visit you next year.	f) wait with pleasure
7 We changed the hotel booking when several extra visitors *turned up*.	g) entertain
8 It was a shame to *turn down* their invitation to the sales conference.	h) refuse

B Tick the correct sentences. Correct the mistakes in the other sentences.

1 She turned me down.
2 Her secretary looks her after really well.
3 I looked the warehouse around.
4 They took us out to an excellent restaurant.
5 The visitors turned very late up.

C Complete this story with the multi-word verbs given below.

I was really worried when I had to meet our new sales team in Tokyo as it was my first time there. No one …*turned up*…¹ at the airport to meet me. Sachiko, the person meeting me, had been given the wrong information. When we finally met, she ………………² me really well. The next day we ………………³ the retail outlets, and I actually ………………⁴ their sales meeting on the last day. In the evening the sales team offered to ………………⁵ for dinner, but I had to ………………⁶ because I was really tired. However, I'm really ………………⁷ my next visit, and I'll certainly ………………⁸ their offer of dinner next time.

1	a) looked around	b) turned up	c) turned down
2	a) looked around	b) looked forward to	c) looked after
3	a) looked around	b) looked forward to	c) looked after
4	a) took care of	b) took part in	c) took up
5	a) take me out	b) look after me	c) turn me down
6	a) take care of them	b) turn them down	c) turn up
7	a) looking after	b) looking forward to	c) looking around
8	a) take up	b) turn up	c) turn down

Skills

Socialising: greetings and small talk

A **What do you say to a business contact when:**

1 you introduce yourself?

2 you introduce another person?

3 you are introduced to another person?

B 🎧 **6.3 Listen to five conversations at a conference. Match up the speakers in each conversation. Then decide whether they know each other.**

Speaker 1	Speaker 2	Do they know each other?
1 Liz	a) Linda Eriksson	....
2 James	b) Jurgen	....
3 Julia	c) Lisa	....
4 John	d) Jane	...*Yes*....
5 Carla	e) Sam Clarke	....

C 🎧 **6.3 Try to complete conversations 2 and 4 below. Then listen again and check your answers.**

Conversation 2

A James, ... *have* ...... you ....¹ Sam Clarke?

B No. Hello, Sam. .... to meet ....² . I think we both ....³ Bill Carlton. I used to ....⁴ with him in Spain.

C Oh, yes ... Bill. He's in Moscow now.

B Really? I didn't know that. .... him my ....⁵ next time you see him.

C Yes, I will.

Conversation 4

A Hi, I'm John.

B Hello, John. ....⁶ to meet you. I'm Lisa from the Munich office.

A Oh, Munich. I've never been, but I ....⁷ it's a ....⁸ city, very lively.

B Yes, it is. It's great. You should come. The conference is going to be there next year.

A I'd ....⁹ to. I'll look ....¹⁰ to it.

D **Look at the expressions below. Which are said by**
a) a host?   b) a guest?

Label each expression either H (for host) or G (for guest).

1 Can I get you a drink?   *H*

2 Yes, it's just down there on the left.

3 It all looks good. What do you recommend?

4 Would you like me to show you round?

5 Help yourself to some food.

6 Yes, please. I'll have a white wine.

7 Can I give you a lift to the airport?

8 Yes, I'd love to see some of the sights.

9 Could you tell me where the toilet is, please?

10 It's very kind of you to offer, but there's a taxi coming for me at 11.00.

E **Match the sentences from Exercise D in logical pairs. For example,**

Can I get you a drink? (1)

Yes, please. I'll have a white wine. (6)

Useful language

Introducing people
Jurgen, this is Lisa.
Anita, do you know Dr Olafson?
Have you met Nigel?
Peter, I'd like you to meet
    Steve Jones.

Making small talk
'How's business?' 'We're having
    a great year.'
'How are things?' 'It's really busy
    at the moment.'

Responding
Pleased to meet you.
Nice to meet you.
Good to see you again.

Requests
Could I use your phone, please?
Do you mind if I take one of
    your brochures?

Offers
Can I give you one of my cards?
Would you like to have dinner
    with us tomorrow night?

F **Work in pairs. Role play the conversation below.**
You are at a conference. You recognise someone you met at a conference two years ago. Introduce yourself and make small talk. Use your role card to prepare for the conversation.

Participant A
- You met B two years ago at a conference on Customer Care in Frankfurt.
- You own a small firm which sells office equipment.
- It's your first day at the conference – you arrived late last night.
- You haven't seen the city yet.
- You are staying at the Grand Hotel in the city centre (a good choice: room service and the facilities are excellent).
- You are leaving in three days' time.
- You think the conference will be very interesting.

Participant B
- You met A two years ago at a conference on Customer Care in Frankfurt.
- You are the sales manager for a large telecommunications company.
- You have been at the conference for three days.
- You have visited the city (beautiful old cathedral, interesting museum, excellent restaurants, but very expensive).
- You are staying at a small hotel outside the city (a bad choice: room too small, too far from the centre of the city).
- You are leaving tomorrow.
- The conference is boring – the speakers talk too much and go overtime.

CASE STUDY

Background

VMI, an international financial services company based in Valencia, Spain, is holding its first international conference later this year. The Chief Executive, senior managers at head office and about fifty managers from its overseas subsidiaries and sales offices will attend. The aims of the conference, in order of priority, are:

- to allow managers to get to know each other and become a stronger international team.
- to thank managers for their hard work.
- to discuss how the company can improve its products and services.

The conference will take place in July. Participants arrive on Friday evening and leave on Monday morning. The budget is $2,000 per participant.

This is an important event and the Marketing Department must plan it carefully. The venue they choose must have:

- reasonable access to an international airport.
- ✓ • one large conference room.
- ✓ • preferably four or more seminar rooms.
- a choice of activities outside the main conference programme.

The marketing team sent out a questionnaire to find out what type of venue the participants preferred. They have selected four to choose from. All prices include the cost of flights.

Preferred location

- Seaside   24
- Out of town   23
- City   28
- Island   25

Task

You are members of VMI's Marketing Department.

1 Work in small groups. Discuss which hotel best meets the requirements of the conference.

2 Meet as one group and listen to each other's ideas.

Writing

As Chief Executive of VMI write an e-mail inviting the overseas sales managers to attend this year's conference. Inform them of the dates, the purpose of the conference and the details of the location.

→ *Writing file page 133*

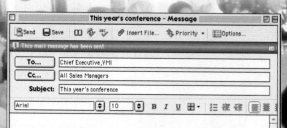

Hotels

1 Long Beach Hotel, Casablanca, Morocco

- Seaside location
- 5-star hotel
- Two large conference rooms but no seminar rooms
- Large swimming pool, sauna, tropical garden, shops and nightclub
- Price: $1,500 per participant, including meals and all entertainment at the hotel (it is a one-hour drive to the town)
- Advantage: Very attractive beach
- Disadvantage: Few cultural attractions

2 Hotel Moda, Prague, Czech Republic

- 4-star hotel
- One conference room and two seminar rooms
- Spacious bedrooms. Large swimming pool (open to the public), sauna, Jacuzzi, hairdressing salon, satellite TV
- Price: $950 per participant, including meals and two guided tours
- Advantage: Low cost means more money for cultural tours, sightseeing, the opera, etc.
- Disadvantages: Half an hour by underground to the city centre. Heavily booked in summer

3 Hotel Matong, Tioman, Malaysia
(an island off the east coast)

- 5-star hotel
- Wide choice of large and small conference rooms
- Spacious grounds with tropical gardens
- Golf course, tennis courts and football pitch
- Price: $1,350 per participant, including meals
- Advantages: Beautiful island setting – peaceful and quiet
- Disadvantage: Not very accessible

4 Hotel Colossus, Las Vegas, USA

- 5-star hotel
- Magnificent architecture in the Greek style
- Huge rooms, with spacious balconies. Own casino
- Outstanding conference facilities. Seminar rooms available at extra cost
- Price $1,950, including meals and one tour. $50 spending money for the casino
- Advantages: Easy access from airport. Many extras such as free use of car included in the price
- Disadvantage: Many tourists visit the hotel day and night.

Revision

4 Great ideas

Verb and noun combinations

Match the verbs 1 to 6 to the nouns that they go with. Then complete the definitions with the phrases a) to f).

If you ...

1	exploit	an award
2	extend	an opportunity *d*
3	win	a range
4	make	a market
5	enter	an opening
6	see	a breakthrough

you ...

a) start selling your products in a new place, or start selling new products.
b) do something more successfully or efficiently than before.
c) see the chance to do something.
d) make the most of a chance to do something.
e) increase the number of products you sell.
f) get a prize because your work is so good.

Reading

Read the text. For each statement 1 to 8 below choose a) right, b) wrong or c) doesn't say.

Juana Lopez has invented a number of things over the years, but they were mostly relatively small improvements to existing products. Then one day she had an idea for a dishwashing machine that worked without using water. She went to see several dishwasher manufacturers about producing the machine, but none of them were interested.

Juana found investors to back her idea and founded her own production company. She spent millions of euros on developing her dishwasher, and it was launched three years later. From the day of the launch, sales were very good – better even than Juana had hoped.

But Global Domestic (GD), one of the companies that she had been to see, launched its own waterless dishwasher. Juana obtained one and found that it used a lot of the technical ideas that she had developed and patented: she had obtained legal protection for these ideas so that other companies could not use them. After a long legal process, GD was forced to stop making its competing dishwasher and to pay Juana several million euros.

Now Juana's waterless dishwasher has 40 percent of the worldwide dishwasher market, and this is increasing every year. There is no other dishwasher like it. Word-of-mouth recommendation by satisfied users has made it a big success.

1 Juana Lopez is Spanish.
2 Her dishwashing machine was her first invention.
3 She went to see several manufacturers about producing the dishwasher.
4 She founded her own production company, entirely with her own money.
5 GD produced a dishwasher that copied a lot of Juana's ideas.
6 Juana's case against GD was settled in a court in the United States.
7 GD was forced to pay Juana for copying her ideas without her permission.
8 Juana's market share of the world dishwasher market was increasing, but now it is getting smaller.

Writing

You work at Classic Appliances (CA). Before Juana Lopez (see page 58) founded her own production company, she came to see you. She discussed with you the possibility of CA manufacturing the waterless dishwasher she had invented. Write a letter (not more than 100 words) to her following your meeting, containing these points:

- thank Juana for coming to see you
- you have discussed the design with colleagues in the research and development department – technical problems with the design – impossible to solve
- people in the marketing department see no demand from consumers for a waterless dishwasher
- CA not interested in manufacturing the product
- thank Juana again for contacting you about the invention – interesting discussion
- wish her luck with future projects
- end suitably

5 Stress

Past simple and present perfect

Look again at the information about using the past simple and the present perfect tenses on page 46. Tick the sentences which are grammatical. Correct the mistakes in the other sentences.

1 Professor Lyall has studied stress for a long time.
2 As a student, she studied psychology.
3 She has done a lot of research on the subject in her mid-20s.
4 She went into companies to interview people.
5 She has finished her first book on stress when she was 29.
6 She became Professor of Psychology at Liverpool University when she was only 32.
7 In the 1990s, Professor Lyall has continued her work on stress by comparing people in different European countries.
8 She wrote another book about stress last year, and it was published in January.

Vocabulary

Complete this article with the correct alternatives.

> ### Stress: a case study
>
> Bea Konrad worked for 15 years as personal assistant to the head of Ajax, a pharmaceutical company. She enjoyed her work despite her heavy ....[1]. She didn't mind the ....[2] : in fact she liked it. She felt she had a lot of freedom in the way she organised her time, as there was a system of ....[3] in the company. Despite having two young children, Bea thought she had a pleasant ....[4].
>
> Then Ajax was taken over by Zenith, another pharmaceutical company. Bea had a new boss who was a ....[5]. He gave out orders and expected everyone to work twice as hard as before for 12 hours a day. The ....[6] became impossible: there was never enough time to finish things. Bea went to see a stress ....[7], who advised her to leave the company. She now works for a firm where everyone leaves at 5.30 p.m. Bea feels much better and more ....[8].

1 **a)** work charge   **b)** workload   **c)** work
2 **a)** press   **b)** pressing   **c)** pressure
3 **a)** elastic time   **b)** stretch time   **c)** flexitime
4 **a)** lifestyle   **b)** life type   **c)** life fashion
5 **a)** workaholic   **b)** work maniac   **c)** work obsessive
6 **a)** deadlines   **b)** lead-times   **c)** delays
7 **a)** counsel   **b)** councillor   **c)** counsellor
8 **a)** relax   **b)** relaxed   **c)** relaxation

Writing

You are Bea Konrad (see previous exercise). Write a letter (70 to 90 words) to your boss, John Hardcastle, explaining why you are leaving Ajax. Include these points:

- say that you are resigning (leaving your job)
- you enjoyed working for Ajax until takeover by Zenith
- pressure now too great
- don't like the pressure and the long hours since the takeover
- increased number of tasks and deadlines – very stressful
- give date you will be leaving (normal period of notice three months, but you want to leave on Friday)
- end suitably

6 Entertaining

Multi-word verbs

Match the verbs 1 to 7 to the nouns that they go with. Then complete the definitions with the phrases a) to g).

If you …

1	call off	a bill
2	cut down on	an event
3	look after	an invitation
4	look round	a house
5	run up	old files
6	take up	cigarettes
7	throw out	a sick person

you …

a) accept it.
b) get rid of them because you no longer need them.
c) cancel it and it does not take place.
d) care for them when they are ill.
e) smoke less than before.
f) spend money that you will have to pay.
g) walk through it, looking at different rooms and the furniture in them.

Choosing a conference centre

Look at the advertisement for a hotel and conference centre. For each item 1 to 7, choose one of the facilities a) to i).

> **PLAZA HOTEL AND CONFERENCE CENTRE FACILITIES**
> **a)** hotel with 100 rooms, including 20 with PCs for Internet access
> **b)** large conference room (200 delegates) with interpreting suite
> **c)** ten smaller conference rooms (up to 40 delegates)
> **d)** Trade Winds Restaurant: international cuisine
> **e)** Typhoon Restaurant: Asian cuisine
> **f)** Monsoon Bar: all cocktails and a selection of 100 Scotch whiskies
> **g)** Hercules Gym Club: fully equipped
> **h)** 3-hour laundry service
> **i)** go-kart track

Choose the facility you are interested in if you want to:

1 drive fast, but not on public roads
2 eat Chinese food
3 get some exercise
4 get your shirts washed quickly
5 have a drink before dinner
6 organise a conference with people speaking different languages
7 stay at the hotel and send e-mails while you are there

Writing

A You organise a conference at the Plaza Hotel and Conference Centre (see page 60). Write a letter (not more than 100 words) to the manager, Melissa Wang, containing these points:

- thank Ms Wang for making the conference a success
- the staff were friendly and helpful
- all equipment in the conference rooms worked
- comment on the quality of the food in the two restaurants and the speed of the service (very important at lunchtime when participants only had 45 minutes for lunch)
- thank Melissa Wang again
- end suitably

B Two years later, you organise another conference at the same hotel, but it is not a success. Write a letter (not more than 100 words) to the new manager, Michael Robinson, about the problems you had.

- you chose the Plaza because of successful conference two years ago, but service not as good this time
- biggest problem: the interpreters from the agency (recommended by the hotel) were not good – this led to misunderstandings and bad feelings
- ask for compensation of some kind
- end suitably

Marketing

❝*Communication is the most important form of marketing.*❞
Akio Morita (1921–1999), Japanese co-founder of Sony

Starting up

A 'The four Ps' form the basis of the *marketing mix*. If you want to market a product successfully, you need to get this mix right.
Match the 'Ps' 1 to 4 to the definitions a) to d).

1	Product	**a)**	the cost to the buyer of goods or services
2	Price	**b)**	informing customers about products and persuading them to buy them
3	Promotion		
4	Place	**c)**	where goods or services are available
		d)	goods or services that are sold

B 🎧 7.1 Listen to four consumers talking about different products. Decide which of the four Ps each speaker is discussing: product, price, promotion or place.

C Think of some products you have bought recently. Why did you buy them? Which of the four Ps influenced your decision to buy?

D Tell your partner about a marketing campaign that impressed you.

Vocabulary
Word partnerships

A For each group of words 1 to 5:
a) fill in the missing vowels.
b) match the words to the definitions a) to c).

1 market	r <u>e</u> s <u>e</u> <u>a</u> rch s _ gm _ nt sh _ re	a) the percentage of sales a company has b) information about what customers want and need c) a group of customers of similar age, income level and social group
2 consumer	b _ h _ v _ _ _ r pr _ f _ l _ g _ _ ds	a) description of a typical customer b) where and how people buy things c) things people buy for their own use
3 product	l _ _ nch l _ f _ cycl_ r _ ng _	a) introduction of a product to the market b) length of time people continue to buy a product c) set of products made by a company
4 sales	f _ r _ c _ st f _ g _ r _ s t _ rg _ t	a) how much a company wants to sell in a period b) how much a company thinks it will sell in a period c) how much a company has sold in a period
5 advertising	c _ mp _ _ gn b _ dg _ t _ g _ ncy	a) a business which advises companies on advertising and makes ads b) an amount of money available for advertising during a particular period c) a programme of advertising activities over a period, with particular aims

B Choose a well-known product for each of these product categories.

1 cars   *Mercedes*
2 newspapers and magazines
3 watches/jewellery
4 clothing

Give typical consumer profiles for each product. Include the following:

- age
- sex
- job
- income level
- other products the consumer might buy

C Consider the products that you described in Exercise B. How could you try to increase their sales?

CASE STUDY

7 Kristal Water

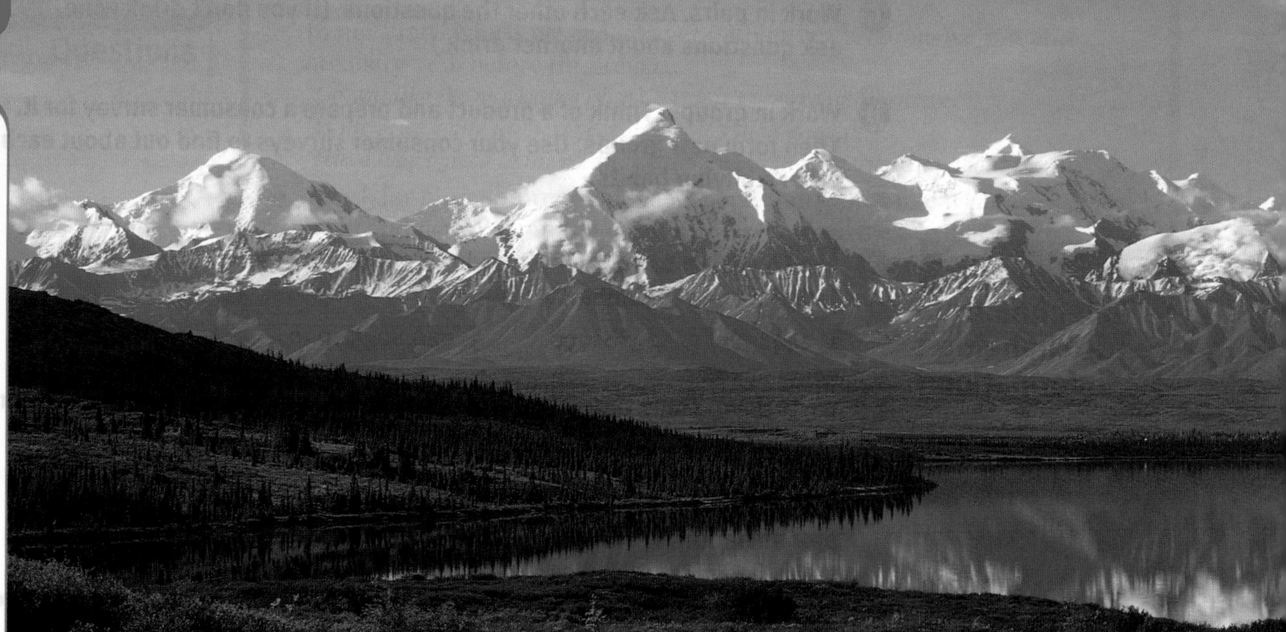

Background

Kristal is a bottled water, manufactured by a US company, Hamilton Food and Drink Products (HFDP). According to HFDP, it comes from a spring deep under the rocks in Alaska, US. It is advertised as the purest water in the world. It has few minerals, and nothing is added to the water to change its taste. The water is targeted at people who want to have a healthy lifestyle.

The launch

Kristal was launched last year in California, US. It was advertised in health magazines with the slogan 'There is no purer drink in the world.' It is sold in clear glass bottles, in 1-litre sizes. Its price is $3, which is higher than most competing brands. The brand name Kristal is printed in large black letters on the label, with a picture of a waterfall. The water is available in delicatessens and health food shops.

After six months, it was clear that the product launch was a failure. Sales were 60% below forecast, and very few people knew that there was a new bottled water product named Kristal.

The Marketing Department interviewed members of the public to find out what was going wrong.

7.9 Listen to some typical comments from consumers. Make notes.

Chart 1: Price comparison

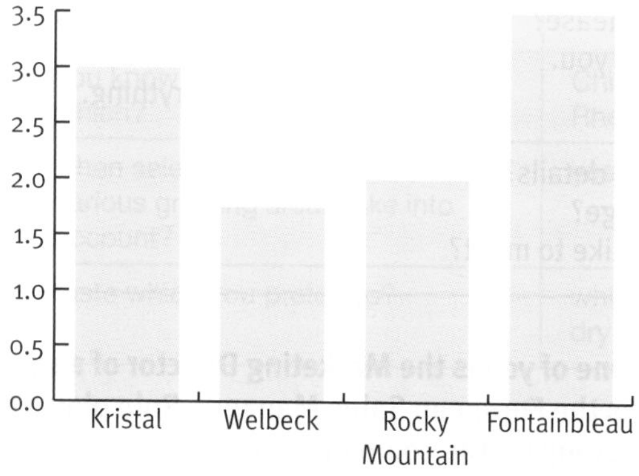

3.5
3.0
2.5
2.0
1.5
1.0
0.5
0.0
Kristal
Welbeck
Rocky Mountain
Fontainbleau

Chart 2: Market share

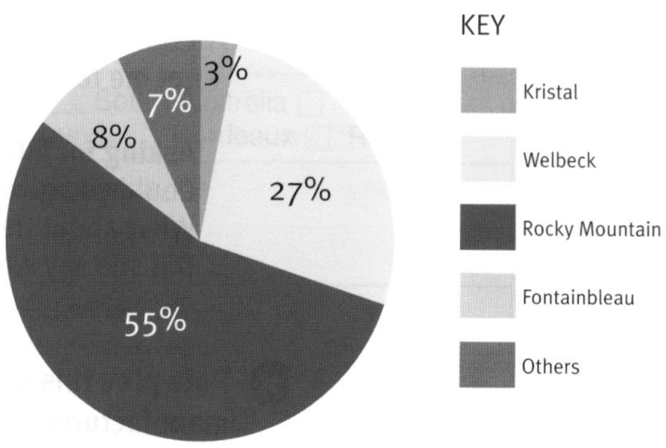

3%
7%
8%
27%
55%
KEY
Kristal
Welbeck
Rocky Mountain
Fontainbleau
Others

Chart 3: Product availability

	Kristal	Welbeck	Rocky Mountain	Fontainbleau
Supermarkets	✗	✓	✓	✗
Health food shops	✓	✗	✓	✓
Convenience stores	✗	✓	✓	✗
Delicatessens	✓	✗	✗	✓

Task

1 Work in groups. Each group is a team in the Marketing Department. Hold a meeting to discuss what you should do to improve sales of Kristal. Use the questions in the box below as a guide.

2 Present your ideas to the other teams in the Marketing Department.

3 As a whole department, hold a meeting and decide what the company must do to improve the sales of Kristal.

Questions

Product: Does the product need to be changed, for example, offer it in a range of sizes?

Price: Is the price correct?

Promotion: Was it promoted in the correct way? Is Kristal targeted at the right segment of the market? If not, who should it be targeted at?

Place: Is it being sold in the right places?

What changes need to be made to relaunch the product?

Writing

As a member of the Marketing Department of HFDP, design a sales leaflet for the campaign to relaunch Kristal Water. The leaflet will be inserted into lifestyle magazines and sent out as part of a direct marketing campaign. It should attract attention and communicate the reasons why people should buy Kristal. It should also include a slogan.

➡ *Writing file* page 134

Planning

PARAMOUNT
présente
UNE PRODUCTION OAKHURST

MICHAEL CAINE et NOEL COWARD
dans
L'OR SE BARRE
avec
BENNY HILL · RAF VALLONE · TONY BECKLEY · ROSSANO BRAZZI
et MAGGIE BLYE
Ecrit par TROY KENNEDY MARTIN · Musique de QUINCY JONES · Produit par MICHAEL DEELEY
Réalisé par PETER COLLINSON
PANAVISION·COULEURS
C'EST UN FILM PARAMOUNT   visa de contrôle N° 3391

❝Plans are nothing; planning is everything.❞
Dwight D Eisenhower (1890–1969), 34th President of the United States

 **Starting up**

A **What do you consider when you plan these things?**

1 a holiday
2 a special family occasion, for example, a wedding
3 an ordinary working day/week
4 your career

B **Which of the following do you use to plan your day or week? Which do you prefer? Why?**

- desk or pocket diary
- ask someone to remind you
- notes stuck on board or fridge
- electronic organiser
- memory
- write on hand

C **Discuss these statements.**

1 Making lists of things to do is a waste of time.
2 You should plan your retirement from an early age.
3 If you make a plan, you should stick to it.

Vocabulary
Ways to plan

A Match the verbs in the box to nouns 1 to 5. Each pair of words describes a way to plan effectively. Use a dictionary to help you.

~~estimate~~ collect consider forecast do

1 ....*estimate*.... costs   4 .... information
2 .... sales   5 .... options
3 .... research

B Match the verbs in the first box to the nouns in the second box. Make as many combinations as you can. For example, *write/implement a plan*.

write   rearrange   meet   arrange   prepare   keep within   implement

a deadline   a schedule   a budget   a plan   a meeting   a report

C A Managing Director talks about the planning of a new sales office in the United States. Complete the text with nouns from Exercises A and B.

Recently we decided to open a new sales office in New York. First I arranged a .... *meeting* ....¹ with the finance department to discuss the project. We prepared a ....² with details of the various costs involved. Then we collected.................³ about possible locations for the new office. We considered two ....⁴ – one in Greenwich Village and the other near Central Park. After doing some more ....⁵, I wrote a ....⁶ for the board of directors.

Unfortunately, we made a mistake when we estimated the ....⁷ as the exchange rate changed, and so we didn't keep within our ....⁸ . We overspent by almost 20 percent. We had to rearrange the ....⁹ for moving into the building because the office was not redecorated in time. The board of directors was unhappy because we didn't meet the ....¹⁰ for opening the office by 15 December. It finally opened in January. However, we forecast ....¹¹ of at least $500,000 in the first year.

D 🎧 8.1 **Now listen and check your answers to Exercise C.**

E Choose one of the following events and tell your partner how you will plan it. Try to use some of the vocabulary from the exercises above.

1 A training weekend for your department
2 A party to celebrate your company's 100th anniversary
3 An event to relaunch a singer's career

The secret of good planning

▲ Rebecca Stephens

A 🎧 **8.2** Rebecca Stephens plans and leads expeditions to the world's highest mountains. In the first part of the interview she talks about the secret of good planning. Listen and complete these sentences.

Rebecca says the secret of good planning is to:

1 know exactly what it is that you want to ....

2 set a ....

3 identify the .... that are necessary.

4 get on with the tasks to a ....

B 🎧 **8.3** In the second part of the interview, Rebecca talks about something she planned well – a project called 'The seven summits'. Listen. Then answer these questions.

1 What did she want to do?

2 Why was time important?

3 What was the key to her planning?

C 🎧 **8.4** Listen to the third part of the interview. Then answer these questions.

1 What is outside our control on a mountain?

2 What is outside our control in business?

3 When things change it is important to:
step ....
reassess the ....
redefine one's ....

4 What is the most important thing according to Rebecca?

D Tell your partner about something you planned well
1 **in business.**   2 **in your life.**
Then tell your partner about something you planned badly.

Planning for tourism

A Match these words to their meanings. Use a good dictionary to help you.

1 a complex
2 inflation
3 devaluation
4 a challenge
5 slum
6 handicrafts
7 facilities
8 infrastructure
9 sanitation
10 a decade

a) things such as pots or baskets which are made at home and sold to tourists

b) a poor area of a city where the houses are in bad condition

c) buildings and equipment that are used for a particular purpose

d) removing sewage and rubbish and providing clean water

e) the speed at which prices increase

f) a goal that is difficult to achieve

g) a reduction in the value of a country's currency

h) a group of buildings that are built close together

i) a period of 10 years

j) things such as transport, communications or banks

B Which of the following words do you associate with Brazil?

beaches   rainforests   tigers   alligators
deserts   jaguars   waterfalls   elephants

C Read the first paragraph of the article and check your answers to Exercise B.

D Read the rest of the article and answer these questions.

1 Where is the Bahia coast?

2 What does Sauipe offer to attract visitors?

3 Who is Sauipe trying to attract?

4 What problems does Brazil face in attracting more tourists?

5 What solutions have been mentioned?

6 What criticisms does Mario Beni make about the new resorts?

7 What do these numbers in the article refer to?

   a) 7,300   **b)** 170 million   **c)** 15   **d)** 2.1 billion

Brazil tries to kick-start tourism

By Geoff Dyer

Brazil has everything to offer the visitor: 7,300 km of coastline, much of it empty, endless beaches; the planet's biggest rainforest; an area of wetlands full of alligators and jaguars; colonial cities and spectacular waterfalls.

The Bahia coast in northeast Brazil is a particularly attractive area for tourism. Several luxury resorts have been built there. Recently a $170 million five-hotel complex at Sauipe opened. With its 18-hole golf course and designer shops, Sauipe is hoping to attract rich, foreign visitors.

The tourist industry had problems in the past because of high inflation which led to short-term planning. Hotels, however, are long-term investments, often with payback periods of over 15 years.

If resorts such as Sauipe are going to attract significant numbers of tourists, they have to solve several problems.

For a start, Brazil needs cheaper and more frequent international air travel. Brazilian airlines have actually decreased the number of scheduled international flights in the past two years because of a currency devaluation.

Foreign visitors also demand a level of service that needs lengthy training – a considerable task for most of the resorts in the northeast which do not have a well-educated population to provide suitable staff.

The other big challenge for Sauipe's managers is to avoid the social problems that other new resorts have caused, when large numbers of people have come from the interior in search of jobs, quickly creating slums.

The resort is hoping to deal with these pressures by setting up courses in the surrounding villages for making handicrafts which will be sold at Sauipe and by organising credit for local co-operatives to produce foodstuffs for the hotels.

Some people believe that the developers have not planned the new resorts properly. 'Sauipe is a resort without adequate infrastructure, training or planning about how the industry will develop,' says Mario Beni, a professor of tourism at the University of São Paulo.

Often created in the middle of nowhere, he says, many of these resorts have poor transport links and no local tourism or sports facilities to take advantage of. 'It is time to stop and think about these grand projects,' he adds.

Not true, replies the Bahia state government, which claims to have spent $2.1 billion over the past decade on basic tourism infrastructure, from roads to airports to sanitation.

From the *Financial Times*

FINANCIAL TIMES
World business newspaper.

E Imagine you are planning a new resort in your own country. Discuss these questions.

1 Where will you build it?

2 What sort of customers will you try to attract?

3 What facilities will you include?

Language review

Talking about future plans

- We can use verbs like *plan, hope, expect, would like* and *want* to talk about future plans.
  *The resort **is hoping** to deal with these pressures.*
  *Brazil **would like** to attract more foreign investors.*
- We often use *going to* to talk about more definite plans.
  *We**'re going to** relaunch the series next year.*
- We can also use the present continuous to talk about definite plans and arrangements.
  *We**'re meeting** next Friday at 3 p.m.*

→ page 125

A **The Managing Director of a Hong Kong–based hotel group is talking to his managers about the group's future plans. Underline the plans that he mentions.**

'Well, I think you all know by now that <u>we're hoping to expand in China</u> and we are going to move our headquarters from Hong Kong to Shanghai. We're planning to manage an executive complex in Dalian and we're also hoping to open a 240-room hotel next year in Zhongshan. We're expecting to make a profit within 5 years although we'd like to break even a bit earlier if possible. Within 10 years we want to become the major international hotel group in Southeast Asia.'

B **Match the verbs to their meanings.**

1 hope	**a)** believe something will happen
2 expect	**b)** decide in detail what you are going to do
3 plan	**c)** wish something will happen

C **A salesperson is talking about the end-of-year bonus. Complete the conversation with verbs from Exercise B.**

I'm ....¹ to get a bonus at the end of the year, but I haven't met all my sales targets, so I'm a little worried. My colleague June has met all her targets and she is ....² to get a good bonus. She is already ....³ to go on an expensive holiday abroad and has got lots of travel brochures.

D **Tell each other about your plans and expectations for 1 to 6 below.**
For example
A *What are you going to do after this lesson?*
B *I'm hoping to/planning to ... . What about you?*
A *Oh, I'm hoping to ...*

1 after this lesson	**4** on your next holiday
2 in the near future	**5** in your career
3 this weekend	**6** when you retire

Meetings: interrupting and clarifying

A 🎧 **8.5 Listen to a meeting in which members of a planning group discuss relocating their head office. In which order are these points mentioned?**

a) the cost of moving ☐

b) when to move ☑

c) the advantage of using a specialised firm ☐

d) whether to use their own transport department ☐

e) how to communicate with staff ☐

f) which transport company to use ☐

B **Look at the extracts from the planning meeting in Exercise A. Decide whether each underlined expression is: a) interrupting or b) clarifying.**

1 B I think July would be the best time. It's very quiet then, isn't it?
   A <u>You mean, we don't do too much business then?</u>

2 C <u>Could I just say something?</u>

3 C In my opinion, we should do it department by department.
   B <u>How do you mean exactly?</u>

4 B We've contacted two companies, National Transport and Fox Removals.
   A <u>Sorry, could I just comment on that, Mark?</u>

5 B You know, there's another possibility. We could get our own people to do the moving.
   A <u>What? You think our transport department could do the job?</u>

C **Role play this situation. The head of your department is leaving the company in a month's time. Your department plans to hold a farewell party. Discuss these questions with other members of the department.**

1 When and where will the party be? At work, in a restaurant or at another location?

2 How much should each member of staff contribute towards the cost of the party?

3 What sort of gift should you get? Who will present it?

4 Will there be a speech? If so, who will make it? Should it be serious or humorous? How long will it be?

5 What kind of entertainment will you have at the party?

6 What else do you need to plan?

Useful language

Interrupting	Clarifying
Could I say something?	How do you mean exactly?
Could I just comment on that?	What exactly do you mean by ...?
Hold on a minute.	Are you saying ...?
Sorry to interrupt but ...	So what you're saying is that ...

The voice of business

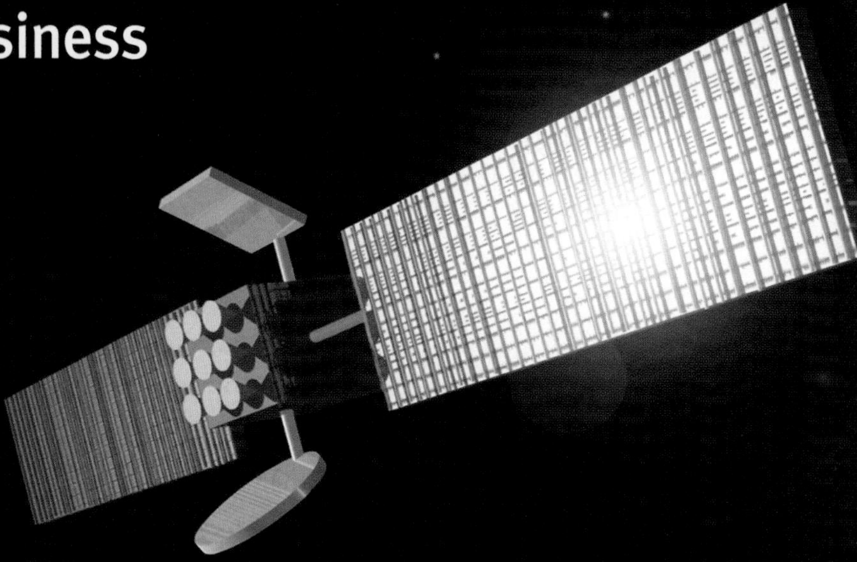

Background

European Business Associates (EBA) is a media company which makes radio and television programmes for broadcasting organisations all over the world. They have won a contract to produce a 30-minute radio programme aimed at working people. It will be broadcast throughout Europe, in English, at 7.00 a.m. three times a week.

Planning

EBA is about to plan its first programme. Recently it sent questionnaires to businesspeople, asking them what they would like in it. People were asked whether they thought topics were a) very interesting, b) quite interesting or c) not interesting. The results are given below.

Chart 1: Interest in possible topics for the radio programme

Topics	Very interesting	Quite interesting	Not interesting
Company profiles	66%	15%	19%
Profiles of businesspeople	45%	12%	43%
Interviews with businesspeople	61%	22%	17%
Business update	72%	19%	9%
The future of business	25%	18%	57%
Investment advice (stock market tips)	36%	28%	36%
Book reviews	25%	32%	43%
Economic reports on countries	24%	35%	41%
Advice on personal finance	68%	11%	21%
Job vacancies	70%	18%	12%
Traffic and weather reports	52%	35%	13%

In addition to using questionnaires, EBA held focus groups in a number of European countries. These were some of the most common opinions.

1 'I want to know what the important news stories will be for that day. You know, what companies are publishing their annual results, that sort of thing. Up-to-date news on what's going on in business.'

2 'You only need one person to present the programme. Male or female, it doesn't matter. But they should be an experienced business journalist.'

3 'I'm interested in buying shares. I'd want some good tips. What to buy, what to sell – that'd be really interesting.'

4 'It would be great if you could give us weather and traffic reports. I'm always getting stuck in a traffic jam.'

🎧 8.6 Now listen to some other common opinions which were recorded at the focus groups. Make notes.

Task

Work in groups. You are members of the EBA planning team. You must plan the first programme. Use the key questions below to help you.
1 Discuss the key questions.
2 Then discuss any other ideas that you have.
3 Agree on a final plan for the first programme.

Key questions
- What will be the main components of the programme?
- How long, approximately, will each component be?
- What will be the order of the various items?
- Who should present the programme?
  Should there be one or two presenters?
  male or female? young or old?
- Should there be live interviews with business personalities?

Writing

As the producer of the new EBA business news programme, write a letter to a famous businessperson asking them for an interview. At the start of the letter you should introduce yourself and give brief details of the programme and its aims.

➡ *Writing file* page 130

Dear ...

I am writing to you as the producer of the exciting new EBA business news programme.
...

UNIT 9
Managing people

❝Management problems always turn out to be people problems.❞

John Peet, British Management Consultant

Starting up

A What qualities and skills should a good manager have? Choose the six most important from the list.

To be a good manager you need to:

1 like people.

2 enjoy working with others.

3 give orders.

4 listen to others.

5 make suggestions.

6 judge people's abilities.

7 plan ahead.

8 be good with numbers.

9 make good presentations.

10 be persuasive.

B If you are managing people from different cultures, what other qualities and skills do you need?

Listening
Good managers

▲ Kriengsak Niratpattanasai

A 🎧 **9.1** **Kriengsak Niratpattanasai is a management consultant in Thailand. Listen to the first part of the interview and complete the chart.**

Managers need to be good at ...	... in order to
1 observing	..*understand*.. the behaviour, the .... and .... of their staff.
2 listening	.... their staff's ....
3 asking questions	.... all the .... they need to make the right decisions.
4 speaking	.... their .... clearly to all their staff.

B 🎧 **9.2** **Listen to the second part of the interview. Decide whether these statements are true or false, according to Kriengsak.**

Managers need to:

1 plan in advance.

2 find out about the local language, culture and conditions.

3 get to know the local people.

4 try to become experts as soon as possible.

5 spend time observing and asking questions.

C 🎧 **9.3** **Listen to the third part of the interview and answer these questions.**

1 What do foreign managers often want from Asian staff?

2 What do the managers sometimes ignore?

3 Why might the managers underestimate the local skills and abilities?

D **What advice would you give to a foreign manager who is going to manage staff in your country?**

Vocabulary
Verbs and prepositions

A Verb and preposition combinations are often useful for describing skills and personal qualities. Match the verbs 1 to 7 with the prepositions and phrases a) to g).

A good manager should:

1	respond	a)	*in* their employees' abilities.
2	listen	b)	*to* a deputy as often as possible.
3	deal	c)	*to* employees' concerns promptly.
4	believe	d)	*with* colleagues clearly.
5	delegate	e)	*with* problems quickly.
6	communicate	f)	*in* regular training courses for employees.
7	invest	g)	*to* all suggestions from staff.

B Which do you think are the three most important qualities in Exercise A?

C Some verbs combine with more than one preposition. For example:
'He <u>reports to</u> the Marketing Director.' (to a person)
'The Sales Manager <u>reported on</u> last month's sales figures.' (on a thing)
Say whether the following combine with *someone* or *something*.

		Someone	Something
1	a) report to	✓	
	b) report on		✓
2	a) apologise for		
	b) apologise to		
3	a) talk to		
	b) talk about		
4	a) agree with		
	b) agree on		
5	a) argue about		
	b) argue with		

D Complete these sentences with suitable prepositions from Exercise C.

1 I agreed ......*with*...... her that we need to change our marketing strategy.
2 I talk .... my boss every Monday at our regular meeting.
3 We argued .... next year's budget for over an hour.
4 He apologised .... losing his temper.
5 We talked .... our financial problems for a long time.
6 The Finance Director argued .... our Managing Director over profit sharing.
7 I apologised .... Paula for giving her the wrong figures.
8 Can we agree .... the date of our next meeting?

E Write three questions using some of the verb and preposition combinations above. Then work in pairs. Ask each other the questions.

A Many US managers are sent abroad to work; some find it difficult to adapt to local conditions. What do you think the figure is?
1 approximately 1 in 7
2 approximately 1 in 5
3 approximately 1 in 3
Now read the article and check your answer.

B Answer these questions about the article.
1 Why has the number of people working abroad increased?
2 Who did the following – the German manager in England or the American manager in France?
   a) He made staff stay inside the building at lunchtime. *German manager*
   b) He gave staff targets.
   c) He had meals with each member of staff.
   d) He stopped staff drinking during working hours.
   e) He seemed to be watching his staff.
   f) He worked harder than other staff.
3 What are the differences in the way the two managers managed their staff?

The **international** manager

IN RECENT YEARS, many companies have expanded globally. They have done this through mergers, joint ventures and co-operation with foreign companies. Because of this globalisation trend, many more employees are working abroad in managerial positions or as part of a multicultural team.

Although it is common nowadays for staff to work abroad to gain experience, many people have difficulty adapting to the new culture. The failure rate in US multinationals is estimated to be as high as 30% and it costs US business $3 billion a year.

Two typical failures have been described in the journal *Management Today*. The first example concerns a German manager with IBM who took up a position as product manager in England. He found that at most lunchtimes and especially on Fridays, many members of staff went to the pub. 'I stopped that right away,' he says. 'Now they are not allowed off the premises. It didn't make me very popular at the time but it is not good for efficiency. There is no way we would do that in Germany. No way.'

The second example is about an American manager who came to France on a management assignment. He was unable to win the trust of his staff although he tried all kinds of ways to do so. He set clear goals, worked longer hours than everybody, participated in all the projects, visited people's offices and even took employees out to lunch one by one. But nothing seemed to work. This was because the staff believed strongly that the management were trying to exploit them.

The German manager's mistake was that he hadn't foreseen the cultural differences. IBM had a firm rule about drinking during working hours. It was not allowed. He didn't understand that staff in other countries might be more flexible in applying the rule.

The American manager used the ways he was familiar with to gain the staff's trust. To them, he seemed more interested in getting the job done than in developing personal relationships. By walking around and visiting everyone in their offices, perhaps he gave the impression that he was 'checking up' on staff. His managerial approach strengthened their feeling of exploitation.

When managers work in foreign countries, they may find it difficult to understand the behaviour of their employees. Moreover, they may find that the techniques which worked at home are not effective in their new workplace.

From *Managing Across Cultures*
by Schneider and Barsoux

C Match words from each column to make common word combinations. For example, *adapt to a new culture*. Then check your answers in the article.
1 adapt to   **a)** rules
2 take up   **b)** relationships
3 set   **c)** goals
4 apply   **d)** a position
5 develop   **e)** a new culture

Language review
Reported speech

There are a number of ways to report what people say.

1 We often use *say*, *tell* and *ask* to report speech.

   'The new job is challenging.' She **said** (that) the new job was challenging.

   • We use *tell* with an object.

   'The new job is challenging.' She **told** her **boss** (that) the new job was challenging.

   • We use *ask* (with or without an object) to report questions.

   'When do you want to start?' Her boss **asked** (**her**) when she wanted to start.

2 We usually make the following changes in reported speech.

   • The verb goes back one tense.

   • Nouns and pronouns may change.

   'My new sales team is difficult to manage.' He said (that) **his** new sales team **was** difficult to manage.

3 When we report things that are either very recent or generally true, we often use the same tense as the speaker.

   'I want to see Pierre.' Pierre, Susan has just phoned and says she **wants** to see you.

   'Training is important.' He said (that) training **is** important. ➜ page 126

A Complete these sentences with the correct form of *say* or *tell*.

1 He ......*said*...... that he was finding it difficult to manage people.

2 He .... me that he was finding it difficult to manage people.

3 She .... him to improve his performance.

4 She .... they would never agree.

5 My boss .... me not to pay the invoice.

6 He .... that he worked for General Electric.

B Use *say*, *tell* and *ask* to report this dialogue between two company directors. For example, *Philip told Amanda/said (that) he wanted to motivate their managers more.*

Philip	I want to motivate our managers more.
Amanda	Are you delegating the less important decisions?
Philip	I think so. And I'm making more time to listen to their suggestions.
Amanda	That's good. Responding to their ideas is really important.
Philip	Is the department investing enough in training?
Amanda	Yes, it is. This year's budget is bigger than last year's.

C 🎧 9.4 Your colleague is away and you have been asked to check their voice mail. Listen to each message. Note down who rang and what was said or asked. Then write a short note for your colleague. For example:

Jenny rang about the conference. She said she'd found a hotel with good rates. She asked how many rooms you wanted to book.

Skills
Socialising and entertaining

A Socialising is an important part of good management. When socialising for business in your country, how important are the following?

1 being on time

2 the way people dress

3 how you address people (first names or family names?)

4 giving gifts

5 shaking hands/kissing/hugging/bowing

B 🎧 **9.5 Rachel, who is from the UK, is on a business trip to Russia. Alexandra is a Russian business contact. Listen to their conversation. Then answer these questions.**

1 What does Alexandra invite Rachel to do?   2 Does Rachel accept?

C 🎧 **9.5 Complete this extract from the conversation in Exercise B.**

Rachel   Well, it's very .... [1], Alexandra, but I think I'd like to relax at the hotel tonight .... [2] don't .... [3]. I'm a bit tired, quite honestly.

Alexandra Are you sure? You'd really enjoy it.

Rachel   It's very kind of you, but perhaps .... [4].

D 🎧 **9.6 Marta is being entertained by Sven, who works for the company she is visiting on a business trip to Sweden. Listen to their conversation. Below are the answers to three questions. What were the questions?**

1 Well, Marta, people like to be in the open air.

2 I usually watch television.

3 Well, generally I spend time with my children.

E 🎧 **9.7 Listen to another conversation between Sven and Marta. What did Sven do to entertain Marta?**

F 🎧 **9.7 Listen again. In which order do you hear these sentences?**

a) I'm glad you enjoyed the tour. ☐

b) We'll be in touch soon. ☐

c) I hope you have a good journey back. ☐

d) Thanks for showing me round the city. ☐

e) Thanks very much for your hospitality. ☑

f) I really enjoyed the meal tonight. ☐

G **Role play these situations.**

1 You are having dinner with a business contact who tries to persuade you to try a type of food you hate. Refuse politely.

2 You meet a business contact in a foreign country. Find out the information below. Also, tell them about yourself using a) to d) as a guide.

a) how they spend their weekends

b) where they go for their holidays

c) what they do in the evenings

d) what kinds of hobbies and sports they like

Useful language

Making excuses
It's very kind of you, but ...
I'd like to take it easy/relax if you don't mind.
It's very kind of you, but another time perhaps.

Making conversation
What do you like to do in your spare time?
Where are you going for your holiday this year?
Can you tell me about any interesting places to visit?
What/How about you?

Showing interest
Interesting!
Really?

Saying goodbye/Thanking your host
Thanks very much for your hospitality.
I really enjoyed the meal.
Thanks for showing me round the city/town.
I'll be in touch soon.
Goodbye. All the best.

The way we do things

Background

Just over a year ago, two marine equipment manufacturers, Muller and Peterson, joined together to form a large company called Muller Peterson Marine (MPM). MPM's new sales team was made up of representatives of both companies. It was led by Muller's Sales Manager, and Peterson's Sales Manager became his deputy.

At the end of the first year, it has become clear that the two groups of sales representatives have very different aims, beliefs and ways of working. These are summarised below and on page 85.

Muller sales representatives

- They are ambitious and very competitive. They are mainly interested in increasing their basic salary and commission. They think the company's main aim is to maximise profit. If they do that, the company will be profitable.

- They promise their customers early delivery dates, but the company often cannot meet the dates and the customers complain.

- They send in short sales reports which are often late and incomplete. They usually forget to send written follow-up when customers place an order.

- They are happy with the present system of payment: low basic salary, high commission.

- They keep information about customers to themselves, rather than sharing it with their colleagues.

- They are aggressive when selling and put pressure on customers to buy. For example, they often offer expensive gifts to customers to build up loyalty and to persuade them to place an order. They say that MPM's products are the best in the world.

Peterson sales representatives

- They believe in working as a team and supporting each other. They think the company's aim is to keep the customer happy and to build up good customer relations. If they do that, the company will be profitable.

- They believe that the company should always meet its delivery dates. Therefore they do not promise customers very early delivery.

- They send in well-written, informative reports on or before the deadline. They always provide written follow-up when a customer places an order.

- They would like a higher basic salary and a bonus paid to the team if they exceed their monthly sales target.

- They believe that staff should co-operate at all times and share information about customers with each other. This is the best way to maximise sales.

- Their sales approach is to build up customer loyalty by gaining their trust. They do not put pressure on customers to buy. They let the customer decide if the product is suitable. They do not believe in giving expensive gifts to customers. Gifts should never exceed €30 in value, in their opinion.

Task

The Sales Manager and Deputy Sales Manager decide to hold a meeting with representatives of both groups. The purpose of the meeting is to decide what actions to take so that the sales representatives work together more effectively.

1 Divide into groups:

    Group A   Sales Managers (turn to page 136)
Group B   Deputy Sales Managers (turn to page 137)
Group C   Muller Sales Representatives (turn to page 138)
Group D   Peterson Sales Representatives (turn to page 140)

2 Read your role cards and prepare for the meeting. Use the agenda as a guide for the meeting. It will be led by the Sales Manager and the Deputy Sales Manager.

3 Form new groups with people from groups A, B, C and D. Have a meeting and decide what actions you should take to improve the effectiveness of the sales team.

AGENDA

1 Relations between sales representatives
2 Delivery dates
3 Reports
4 Payment system
5 Sharing information
6 Customer loyalty

Writing

As the Sales Manager of MPM, write a memo to the CEO about the actions agreed on in the meeting with the sales representatives.

➡ *Writing file* page 131

MEMO

To: CEO
From: Sales Manager
Date:
Subject: Improving co-operation
           in the sales department

A meeting was held on ... to discuss how the sales reps could work together more effectively. The following points were agreed:

7 Marketing

A Match the words to make word partnerships.

1 market ——— budget
2 consumer ——— target
3 product ——— leader
4 sales ——— goods
5 advertising ——— launch

B Now match the word partnerships to their definitions.

a) products sold to people for their own use
b) when a new product is introduced
c) the amount of goods a company wants to sell in a particular period
d) the amount of money a company is going to spend on advertising in a particular period
e) the company or product with the most sales

Complete the questions in this questionnaire about holidays. (Look at the answers on the right to help you.) Each slash (/) indicates one or more missing words.

General information

1 / age group / in?	35–40.
2 / have children?	Yes, two boys.
3 / old / they?	The older one is 10 and the other is 8.
4 / much / earn?	$45,000 a year after tax.
5 How / times a year / go on holiday?	Two.
6 / usually go on holiday alone or with friends or your family?	We always go together as a family.

Your last holiday

7 When / your last holiday?	In January.
8 Where / go?	We went skiing in Aspen, Colorado.
9 / buy a package or arrange it yourselves?	We arranged it ourselves.
10 How / travel?	We flew from Chicago to Aspen.
11 / long / go for?	One week.
12 / like and dislike most about the holiday?	The ski facilities were excellent, but there was not enough for the children to do in the evenings.

You work for a market research organisation in the United States. Finish the report about Mr and Mrs Quinn, who have bought a ski holiday.

• Use the questions and answers in the questionnaire above.
• End the report by making a recommendation about how to improve the type of holiday you described for people like Mr and Mrs Quinn (not more than 100 words, not including the part of the report that has already been written for you).

MARKET RESEARCH REPORT

I interviewed Mr and Mrs Quinn about their holidays. They are in the 35 to 40 age group. They have two children, boys aged 8 and 10. Mr and Mrs Quinn both work, and together they earn $45,000 a year after tax. They usually take two holidays a year, one in summer and one in winter. They always take their children.

....

....

....

8 | Planning

Vocabulary   **Complete this text with the correct alternatives.**

Planning: when it all goes right

I work for a US clothes store chain. Last year I was responsible for opening a chain of new shops in Europe. I was very nervous, but I followed the rules: I prepared the ....[1], I fixed a ....[2] for opening dates of stores, and I made some sales ....[3].

Everything went perfectly. We ran a very good advertising ....[4]. The shops were ready ....[5] and the stocks of clothes were all in place on the opening day for each store. We ....[6] our sales targets. In fact, sales were 12 percent ....[7] the forecast I had made. My next forecast? I'm going to be promoted!

---

1 a) account   **b)** budget   **c)** receipts
2 a) scene   **b)** scheme   **c)** schedule
3 a) forecasts   **b)** predictions   **c)** projects
4 a) programme   **b)** campaign   **c)** activity
5 a) in time   **b)** under time   **c)** after time
6 a) went   **b)** arrived   **c)** met
7 a) top   **b)** over   **c)** up

Reading   **Read this report. In each line 1 to 5 there is one wrong word. Underline the wrong word and write the correct word in the space provided.**

Planning for the future

We can make plans for the future, but somehow things never develop in the way we expect they will. Thirty years ago there was a big increase in the price of oil,

1   and companies made plannings based on a future of high oil prices.   ....

2   Companies and individuals hopes to save energy and use less oil, ...

3   but in the long time these plans were not necessary because the   ....

4   oil price has felt and oil is now cheaper than before. Big companies   ....

5   have teams of people who try to forecasted how the situation in   ....
    different countries may develop, and they make different plans for the
    companies' future activities in each country, depending on what happens there.

Report writing

You are regional sales director for a soft drink called Quench. Three years ago you forecast sales in your region for the following years. The three years have now passed.

	Year 1	Year 2	Year 3
Forecast sales (units)	1.5 million	1.7 million	2 million
Actual sales (units)	1.1 million	1.35 million	1.8 million
Main reason	Bad weather during the summer – cold and wet	Good weather during the summer – production difficulties at the factory – could not satisfy demand	Good weather during the summer – strike by delivery drivers in July – more lost sales

Complete the report below for your boss.

The report

- gives figures for forecast and actual sales
- explains the differences between the two sets of figures
- gives conclusions about a) whether the sales department is responsible for the poor sales, and b) how sales can be improved in the future.

The first and third paragraphs have been written for you. Write the second and fourth paragraphs. Each paragraph should be not more than 40 words.

> Three years ago we made a sales forecast for Year 1 of 1.5 million units. Unfortunately, we only had sales of 1.1 million. This was mainly because of the very bad weather we had during the summer – it was very cold and wet, so people did not want to buy soft drinks.
>
> ....
> ....
> ....
>
> For Year 3, we had forecast sales of 2 million units, but a strike by delivery drivers in July meant that again we could not satisfy the demand, and we only had sales of 1.8 million.
>
> ....
> ....
> ....

9 Managing people

Reported speech

Look again at the information about reported speech on page 82.

You work in the central human resources department of an international company. Tell your colleagues about things that have happened today. Put the verbs in brackets into the correct form of the present tense (simple or continuous), as in the example.

1 Susan has just phoned and she (say) that there (be) big problems with the salary payment system.

Susan has just phoned and she says that there are big problems with the salary payment system.

2 Tomas has e-mailed me and he (tell) me that the new American boss (not understand) the way his department (work).

3 Ulla was in here just now and she (complain) that the promotion policies of the company (cause) a lot of unhappiness among the staff.

4 Victor has sent a fax from the Moscow office and he (ask) me to give you his regards.

5 I've just had lunch with Wanda and she (inform) me that the new salespeople we (recruit) for her department are no good.

6 I was on the phone to Xavier just now – he (say) that sales (be) very bad in France and we (have) to make some of the employees there redundant.

7 I ran into Yvonne and Zac downstairs and they (tell) me that the whole company is in big financial trouble.

It is now a week later. Say what happened last week, using the correct verb tenses.

1 Susan phoned and said that there were big problems with the salary payment system.

Reading

Correct this letter to Christine Robinson, a journalist on a newspaper in Jamaica.

In most of the lines 1 to 5 there is one extra word that does not fit. One or two of the lines, however, are correct. If a line is correct, put a tick in the space next to that line. If there is an extra word in the line, write that word in the space.

> Dear Ms Robinson,
>
> I am a 29-year-old secretary working for an American boss, who is very polite and friendly. My salary is excellent. The work is interesting and there are good possibilities for promotion in the company. But I am seriously
>
> 1 considering to resigning. My boss is too direct – he shouldn't
>
> 2 tell people directly what he thinks of them. He works hard
>
> 3 and he rarely takes breaks – he eats a sandwich for the lunch.
>
> 4 When he's away to on a business trip, I want to be sure that
>
> 5 I'm in the office when he is phones, but I also want to take proper breaks and have a proper sit-down lunch away from the office. I miss having a social life in my current job – I think leisure time is more important than my work, even if my job is very good. What can I do?
>
> Yours sincerely,
>
> Janet Jones
>
> Kingston, Jamaica

1 ....
2 ....
3 ....
4 ....
5 ....

Writing

You are Christine Robinson, the newspaper journalist who receives the letter above. Write a letter (not more than 100 words) to Janet Jones that will appear in the newspaper. Your letter should give advice to the secretary on what to do: should she stay or should she leave the company?

❝Why is there no conflict at this meeting?❞

Michael Eisner, American Chairman and CEO of Walt Disney Company

Starting up | How good are you at managing conflict? Answer the questions in the quiz below. Then turn to page 137 to find out. Compare your score with a partner.

1 You are in a meeting. People cannot agree with each other. Do you

a) say nothing?
b) intervene and propose something new?
c) take sides with those you like?
d) suggest a 10-minute break?

2 Your two closest friends have an argument and stop speaking to each other. Do you

a) behave as though nothing has happened?
b) bring them together to discuss the problem?
c) take the side of one and stop speaking to the other?
d) talk to each one separately about the situation?

3 You see two strangers. One begins to hit the other. Do you

a) pretend to be an off-duty police officer, and ask them what is going on?
b) call the police?
c) shout at them to stop?
d) walk away quickly?

4 Your neighbours are playing very loud music late at night. Do you

a) ask them to turn it down?
b) do nothing?
c) call the police?
d) play your own music as loudly as possible?

5 You are in the check-in queue at an airport. Somebody pushes in. Do you

a) ask them to go to the back of the queue?
b) say nothing?
c) complain loudly to everyone about people jumping queues?
d) report them to an airport official?

6 A colleague criticises your work. Do you

a) consider carefully what they say?
b) ignore them?
c) get angry and criticise them?
d) smile, but wait for an opportunity to get back at them?

Listening

Handling conflicts

▲ Jeremy Keeley

A 🎧 10.1, 10.2 **Jeremy Keeley is a management consultant. In the interview he describes a conflict which was handled badly and another which was handled well. Listen to both examples and in each case answer the following questions.**

1 Who was involved?

2 What was the problem?

3 What action did they take?

4 What was the result?

B **Tell your partner about your own experience of:**

1 a conflict which was handled well.

2 a conflict which was handled badly.

Reading

Negotiating across cultures

A **Work in groups of four. You are each going to read an article about a different negotiating style. Choose *either* Article A *or* B below, *or* Article C *or* D on page 92.**

Before you read, match the words from your article with their definitions. Then, as one group, answer the questions in Exercise B on page 92.

Article A

1 tactics

2 make compromises

3 consistency

a) be flexible

b) not changing your opinion or attitude

c) the methods you use to get what you want

Negotiations are demanding and may become emotional. You may find your Russian negotiator 5 banging his or her fist on the table or leaving the room. Accept such tactics with patience and calmness. They are 10 designed to make it difficult for you to concentrate.

Russian negotiating teams are often made up 15 of experienced managers whose style can be like a game of chess, with moves planned in advance. Wanting to 20 make compromises may be seen as a sign of weakness.

Distinguish between your behaviour inside 25 and outside the negotiations. Impatience, tough- ness and emotion during the negotiations should be met with calmness, 30 patience and consistency. Outside the negotiating process you can show affection and personal sympathy.

From the *Financial Times*

FINANCIAL TIMES
World business newspaper.

Article B

1 speak your mind

2 place great weight on

3 exploratory phases

a) when you find out what the other side wants

b) say what you think

c) consider very important

As well as being formal, negotiations are direct. German managers speak 15 their mind. They place 5 great weight on the clarity of the subject matter and get to the point quickly.

Excessive enthusiasm 10 or compliments are rare in German business. You should give a thorough and detailed presenta- tion, with an emphasis 15 on objective information, such as your company's history, rather than on clever visuals or market- ing tricks.

20 Prepare thoroughly before the negotiation and be sure to make your position clear during the opening stage of the talks, as well as during 25 their exploratory phases. Avoid interrupting, unless you have an urgent question about 30 the presentation.

From the *Financial Times*

FINANCIAL TIMES
World business newspaper.

Article C

1 small talk   **a)** style of behaviour
2 protocol   **b)** polite or social conversation
3 manner   **c)** the way things are done on official occasions

Communicating is a natural talent of Americans. When negotiating partners meet, the emphasis is on small talk and smiling. There is liberal use of a sense of humour that is more direct than it is in the UK. Informality is the rule. Business partners do not use their academic titles on their business cards. Sandwiches and drinks in plastic or boxes are served during conferences.

This pleasant attitude continues in the negotiation itself. US negotiators usually attach little importance to status, title, formalities and protocol. They communicate in an informal and direct manner on a first-name basis. Their manner is relaxed and casual.

The attitude 'time is money' has more influence on business communication in the US than it does anywhere else. Developing a personal relationship with the business partner is not as important as getting results.

From the *Financial Times*

FINANCIAL TIMES
World business newspaper.

Article D

1 counterparts   **a)** unplanned thoughts
2 spontaneous ideas   **b)** give your opinion
3 put your point across   **c)** the people on the other negotiating team

At the start of the negotiations you might want to decide whether you need interpreters. You should have documentation available in Spanish. Business cards should carry details in Spanish and English.

During the negotiations your counterparts may interrupt each other, or even you. It is quite common in Spain for this to happen in the middle of a sentence. For several people to talk at the same time is accepted in Latin cultures, but is considered rather unusual in Northern Europe.

The discussion is likely to be lively. In negotiations, Spanish business people rely on quick thinking and spontaneous ideas rather than careful preparation. It may appear that everybody is trying to put his or her point across at once. That can make negotiations in Spain intense and lengthy, but also enjoyably creative.

From the *Financial Times*

FINANCIAL TIMES
World business newspaper.

B **Work in your groups to answer these questions.**

In which country (Russia, Germany, the US or Spain):

1 should you start a negotiation with general conversation?

2 do negotiators show strong emotions?

3 is it common for there to be several conversations at the same time during a negotiation?

4 do negotiators focus on results rather than developing relationships?

5 do negotiators plan their tactics carefully?

6 should you not stop someone while they are talking?

7 is it usual for the atmosphere to be relaxed and friendly?

8 do negotiators prefer to think of ideas during a negotiation rather than before it starts?

9 do negotiators like to talk about business immediately?

10 should you not give the other side too much as they will not respect you?

C **Discuss these questions.**

1 If you are from one of the countries in the articles, do you agree with what the article says?

2 If you are from another country, which of the countries is the nearest to your own country in terms of negotiating behaviour? Why?

Vocabulary
Word building

A Use the correct form of these words from the articles to complete the first two columns of the chart. Use a good dictionary to help you.

	Noun	Adjective	Opposite
1	patience	...*patient*......	....
2	calmness	....	nervous
3	weakness	....	strong
4	toughness	....	....
5	emotion	....	....
6	consistency	....	....
7	sympathy	....	....
8	....	formal	informal
9	enthusiasm	....	....
10	....	creative	....

B Opposite meanings of the adjectives above are formed in one of two ways:
a) using a prefix un-, in-, im-; for example, *formal, informal*.
b) using a different word; for example, *weak, strong*.
Complete the right-hand column of the chart with opposites of the adjectives.

C Use one of the adjectives or its opposite to complete the following sentences.

1 He gets very angry if people are late for negotiations.
He is very ...*impatient*.... .

2 She always has ideas and easily finds solutions to problems.
She is a very .... person.

3 He never shows anger, enthusiasm or disappointment during a negotiation.
He is totally ....

4 He always agrees with everything his negotiating partner suggests.
He is ....

5 She wants to get her own way. She doesn't like to compromise.
She is a very .... negotiator.

6 He likes people to feel comfortable and relaxed during a negotiation.
An .... atmosphere is very important to him.

D Look again at the adjectives and their opposites. Choose what you think are the best and worst qualities for a negotiator. Then compare your ideas with a partner and try to reach an agreement.

Language review
Conditionals

- **First conditional**
  if + present simple, *will* + base form of the verb
  This describes a possible condition and its probable result. It is often used to make promises.
  *If we **meet** our sales target, we'**ll get** a bonus.*

- **Second conditional**
  if + past simple, *would* + base form of the verb
  This describes an unlikely condition and its probable result. It is often used to discuss options.
  *If he **listened** more, he'**d be** a better manager.*

- **Conditionals and negotiating**
  Conditionals are often used when negotiating.
  *If you **give** us an 8% discount, we'**ll make** a firm order.*

page 127

A **Correct the grammatical mistakes in the sentences below.**

1 If you give us a 10% discount, we would place our order today.
2 If I would have more money, I would go on a cruise.
3 If I will go to London next week, I'll visit their sales office.
4 If I would work from home, I would have more time with my children.

B **Combine phrases from columns A and B to make conditional sentences. For example, *If you pay in euros, we'll deliver within seven days*. More than one answer may be possible in each case.**

A	B
1 pay in euros	a) pay you a higher commission
2 order today	b) offer you a special discount
3 finish everything tonight	c) reduce the price
4 deliver by the end of the month	d) give you a signing-on bonus
5 give us a one-year guarantee	e) pay all the transport costs
6 exceed the sales target	f) give you a 5% discount
7 pay all the advertising costs	g) deliver within seven days
8 sign the contract now	h) give you the day off tomorrow

C **Discuss the following questions in pairs.**

What would you do if:

1 you saw two colleagues having an argument? *I wouldn't get involved.*
2 a colleague criticised you?
3 you saw a colleague stealing something?
4 your boss never listened to your ideas?
5 your boss asked you to work till midnight?

What would you do if you saw two colleagues having an argument?

Skills

Negotiating: dealing with conflict

A **Which of the following are good ways of dealing with conflict in a negotiation?**

1 Avoid eye contact.
2 Smile a lot.
3 Sit back and appear relaxed.
4 Stop the discussion and come back to it later.
5 Say nothing for a long time.
6 Say 'I see what you mean.'
7 Find out why the other side is unhappy.
8 Focus on the issues, not on personalities.
9 Say something humorous.
10 Speak calmly and slowly.

B 🎧 **10.3 A union representative meets a general manager. The representative is angry because the company's staff are no longer allowed to use the company car park. Listen to the conversation and answer the questions.**

1 What is the general manager's first suggestion to solve the problem?
2 Why does the union representative reject the suggestion?
3 What solution do they finally agree on?

C 🎧 **10.3 Listen again and complete the extracts.**

1 Look, Tracy, I ..*understand*.. what you're .... , but it just isn't possible anymore.
2 We've got to do something about it. OK, ... this? .... we keep five spaces for staff, and it's first come, first served?
3 There is another .... How about if the staff park their cars in the car park near the station?
4 OK, Tracy. What if we .... help towards the cost? We .... be able to pay, say, 30 percent.

D **Discuss whether the extracts in Exercise C are examples of *calming people down* or *creating solutions*.**

Useful language

Calming down
I understand what you're saying.
I can see your point of view.
Well, I know/see what you mean.
Why don't we come back to that later?
Let's have a break and come back with some fresh ideas.
You don't have to worry about ...

Closing a negotiation
Let's see what we've got.
Can I go over what we've agreed?
Let's go over the main points again.
OK, I think that covers everything.
We've got a deal.
Fine. Right. That's it then.

Creating solutions
A compromise could be to ...
How about if ...
What if ...
Let's look at this another way.
Another possibility is ...

E **Work in pairs. Role play this situation.**

One day staff find that prices have risen by over 50% in the staff restaurant. This is because the company has stopped subsidising all drinks and meals. Their union representative meets the general manager to discuss the situation.
You are *either*:
the union representative (turn to page 140) *or*
the general manager (turn to page 142).

CASE STUDY

Background

Todd Foster became Marketing Manager of European Campers a year ago. The company, which was founded by Charles Holden, its Chief Executive, is based in Bordeaux, France. It makes and sells camping and outdoor equipment.

Todd, aged 34, is an American with a Master's in Business Administration (MBA). Since Todd joined the company two years ago, profits have risen dramatically and the company is enjoying great success.

A problem with the top salesman

Olivier Moyon has three sales areas: France, Spain and Italy. He has been with the company 12 years, and everyone agrees that he is a brilliant salesman. His results are outstanding. In fact, the sales from his areas amount to 24% of the firm's total sales. Unfortunately, however, Olivier is very difficult to manage. Todd cannot control him properly and this is causing problems.

Here are some examples of Olivier's unacceptable behaviour.

- Olivier spends far too much money on entertainment and gifts for his customers. His expenses are much higher than all the other representatives.

- He only sent five sales reports last year instead of sending twelve (one each month).

- He crashed his company car. He blamed bad road conditions, but Todd believes he had drunk too much alcohol.

- He has still not introduced Todd to the biggest buyers in his areas. He says the buyers are too busy to meet Todd.

- He often does not call back when Todd leaves messages on Olivier's mobile phone.

- He has missed several important meetings, saying that he is unwell or 'feels stressed'.

Conflict

Two weeks ago, Olivier got a large order from a department store chain for some camping tables and chairs. However, the equipment had to be delivered by the end of the month, at the latest. When he telephoned the Production Manager, Jacques Picard, to arrange delivery of the goods, Jacques told him that he could not produce the goods and deliver them by that date. Olivier became very angry and was extremely rude to him. Jacques complained to Todd about Olivier's behaviour. Jacques explained that a very good customer had also placed an order for some tables and chairs, and this order had to be given priority. Jacques ended the conversation by saying, 'Olivier may be a good salesman, but no one likes him here. He's rude and cares only about himself. He's impossible to work with.'

Task

1 You are negotiating as either:
   - Charles Holden, Chief Executive (turn to page 137) or
   - Todd Foster, Marketing Manager (turn to page 139).

   You disagree about how to handle the problem with Olivier Moyon. Try to negotiate a suitable solution. Read your role card, prepare for your meeting and then negotiate a solution to the problem.

2 Meet as one group and compare the decisions you have taken. Try to persuade your colleagues that your solution was the best.

Todd Foster meets Olivier Moyon

🎧 **10.4** At the beginning of the week, Olivier arranged to meet Todd at the head office in Bordeaux. Listen to this extract from their conversation. Make notes.

Writing

You are Head of Personnel at European Campers. Write a letter to Olivier Moyon, informing him of the result of the meeting between Charles Holden and Todd Foster.

 *Writing file* page 130

European Campers
100 avenue de la République
33405 Bordeaux

Dear Mr Moyon

I am writing to inform you of the outcome of the recent meeting between Charles Holden and Todd Foster. ...

11 New business

> *There is always plenty of business, if you are smart enough to get it.*
>
> E W Howe (1853–1937)
> American writer

Starting up

A What conditions are important for people starting new businesses? Choose the *three* most important from this list. Can you think of any others?

- low taxes
- skilled staff
- low interest rates
- cheap rents
- stable economy

- good transport links
- training courses
- high unemployment
- a strong currency
- government grants

B Many economies contain a mix of public and private sector businesses. Think of companies you know in the areas below. Which are public sector companies and which are private sector companies?

- post office
- TV/newspapers
- energy
- cars

- rail
- water
- telecoms
- airlines

C Many companies in the UK have been privatised recently. What are the trends in your country? Talk about the business sectors in Exercise B.

Vocabulary
Economic terms

A Match the economic terms 1 to 10 to their definitions a) to j).

1 interest rate
2 exchange rate
3 inflation rate
4 labour force
5 tax incentives
6 government bureaucracy
7 GDP (gross domestic product)
8 unemployment rate
9 foreign investment
10 balance of trade

a) total value of goods and services produced in a country
b) general increase in prices
c) cost of borrowing money
d) price at which one currency can buy another
e) percentage of people without jobs
f) people working
g) low taxes to encourage business activity
h) money from overseas
i) official rules/regulations/paperwork
j) difference in value between a country's imports and exports

B Try to complete this economic profile without looking back at the terms in Exercise A.

The economy is stable following the problems of the past two years. By following a tight monetary policy the government has reduced the _inflation_.... _rate_.........[1] to 2%. After going up dramatically, the _i_............. _r_..............[2] is now down to 8%. The last six months has seen a slight improvement in the _e_............. _r_..............[3] against the dollar. The _G_.............[4] has grown by 0.15%. Exports are increasing and the _b_............. of _t_.............[5] is starting to look much healthier.

The _u_............. _r_.............[6] continues to be a problem as it is still 16%. In order to stimulate the economy and attract _f_............. _i_.............[7] the government is offering new _t_............. _i_.............[8] as well as making a renewed effort to reduce _g_............. _b_.............[9]. Finally, a large skilled _l_............. _f_.............[10] means there could be attractive investment opportunities over the next five years.

C 11.1 Listen to the report and check your answers to Exercise B.

D Write sentences about the economic profile of your country.

Listening
Starting new businesses

▲ Yvonne Thompson

A 🎧 11.2 **Yvonne Thompson provides advice for people who are starting new businesses. Listen to the first part of the interview and complete this extract.**

When you're starting your own company, you have to be very . *confident* .¹. You have to be very ....² . You have to know what it is you're doing. You need to ....³ the business – or the business arena that you're intending to go into. You need to research your ....⁴ and benchmark your ....⁵ or your product against your competitors. You need good family ....⁶ . You need good backup from your friends. And probably the most important thing is that you need a good mentor, and that needs to be a ....⁷ mentor as well as a ....⁸ mentor.

B 🎧 11.3 **Listen to the second part of the interview. Which of the following points does Yvonne say are important?**
- business plan
- relationship with your bank
- economic conditions
- workforce
- marketing campaign

Reading
Developing a new industry

A **The article on page 101 describes a major new industry which has developed in Sicily. What do you think it is?**

B **Read the first two paragraphs of the article and answer these questions.**
1 Which industry is the article about?
2 Who is Pasquale Pistorio?
3 How big is his company?

C **Read the rest of the article and answer these questions.**
1 Which other high-tech centre is compared to Etna Valley? How are the two places similar?
2 Who provided incentives to invest in Catania?
3 Why are high-tech companies keen to set up businesses in Catania?

D **Find words in the article with the meanings below.**
1 changed completely (paragraph 1)   *transformed*
2 trying hard to be more successful than others (paragraph 2)
3 the things you need to make something (paragraph 3)
4 things which are used to encourage people (paragraph 4)
5 factory (paragraph 5)
6 a company's equipment, buildings and services (paragraph 6)
7 were better or greater than (paragraph 7)

E **Choose an area in your country. Explain why it would be a good location for:**
a) a high-tech start-up company.
b) a start-up company of your choice.

Success in the shadow of Etna

By Paul Betts

The Sicilian port city of Catania, dominated by Mount Etna, Europe's biggest active volcano, is being transformed into a Mediterranean Silicon Valley. And the 'Etna Valley', as it is already being called, is rapidly changing the old stereotype image of the island at the tip of Italy.

'Catania has become the most competitive place in Europe for high-tech investments,' argues Pasquale Pistorio, the Sicilian chairman of ST Microelectronics. This Franco-Italian group has rapidly grown to become Europe's largest and the world's number six, after the likes of Intel, Toshiba and Motorola, under Mr Pistorio's leadership.

A former Motorola senior executive, he invested in Catania because he felt from the start that the Sicilian city had all the ingredients to develop into a competitive high-tech centre. Like California's Silicon Valley, the city had a good university working closely with a leading enterprise. In turn, this provided the basis for stimulating new entrepreneurial, research and academic activities.

Although Italy's deep south is not California, incentives provided by the European Union, the Italian government and local organisations, as well as Mr Pistorio's personal commitment, helped Catania grow into a high-technology centre.

Mr Pistorio remembers when he first joined the company 20 years ago. The Catania plant was losing a lot of money. But the island also had a well-educated population and offered high-tech companies what Mr Pistorio calls 'ample brain power resources'.

When there are few jobs, young people tend to study more. Thanks partly to its high unemployment rate, the island had a large supply of intellectual labour. And Mr Pistorio encouraged studying with ST Microelectronics working with Catania University, running advanced courses in its facilities and employing many of the graduates.

Thanks to the high rate of unemployment and government and EU incentives, Mr Pistorio quickly found that brain-power cost significantly less in Sicily than elsewhere in Europe. The results have exceeded all expectations.

From the *Financial Times*

FINANCIAL TIMES
World business newspaper.

Language review
Time clauses

Time clauses provide information about actions and events in the past, present and future.

1 We often use *when* to introduce time clauses.
- *Mr Pistorio remembers **when** he first joined the company ... .* (past time)
- ***When** there are few jobs, young people tend to study more.* (present time)
- ***When** I'm on the plane, I'll read all the contracts.* (future time)

2 We can also use *while, before, after, until* and *as soon as* to introduce time clauses.
- *Many new high-tech companies started **while** the economy was growing.*
- *We need to arrange our finance **before** we can develop the business.*
- ***After** we meet the candidates we'll decide how many to employ.*
- ***Until** inflation is under control, planning will be difficult.*

3 When we use a time clause to talk about the future, the verb in the time clause is in the present tense or the present perfect tense.
- ***As soon as** they **sign** the contract, we'll announce the deal.*
- *We'll make the decision **when** we**'ve finished** the budget.* ➡ page 128

A Match the sentence halves to make appropriate sentences.

1 We'll have breakfast in the hotel
2 Please talk to your line manager
3 Until we have full employment,
4 We won't hire new staff
5 While you're waiting for the fax,
6 We can set up in that country
7 While I'm with this company,
8 Consumer spending rises

a) could you check these figures.
b) when the conditions are right.
c) as soon as interest rates fall.
d) until we get new business.
e) before you sign the contract.
f) our economy will not improve.
g) before we go to the office.
h) I want opportunities for training.

B Complete these sentences with *when, while, before, after, until* or *as soon as*. More than one answer may be possible in each case.

1 Don't make a decision .... we've seen the report.
2 I'm meeting with Atsuko this afternoon. Send her up .... she arrives.
3 Let's sort out this problem .... she gets here.
4 I'm coming to Paris tomorrow afternoon. I'll phone you .... I arrive.
5 Can you type this report for me .... I'm away?

C Kate North is an American who works in London. Read about her work routine and underline the most appropriate words.

I usually get to work *before* / *as soon as* / *until* [1] my boss arrives and *as soon as* / *while* / *before* [2] I arrive I check my e-mail and post. I usually try to answer all important enquiries *until* / *as soon as* / *before* [3] I go to lunch. *As soon as* / *Until* / *While* [4] I'm having lunch, I often discuss problems with colleagues. *When* / *Before* / *Until* [5] I work long hours, I can take time off another day. I have a lot of flexibility over *as soon as* / *when* / *until* [6] I arrive at the office and *before* / *when* / *while* [7] I leave, depending on the daily workload.

D 🎧 11.4 Listen to the recording and check your answers.

▲ Kate North

Skills

Dealing with numbers

A 🎧 **11.5 Say these numbers. Listen and check after each group.**

1 **a)** 47   **b)** 362   **c)** 1,841   **d)** 15,000   **e)** 36,503
   f) 684,321   **g)** 4,537,295

2 **a)** 3.5   **b)** 2.89   **c)** 9.875

3 **a)** $\frac{3}{4}$ **b)** $\frac{1}{8}$ **c)** $\frac{6}{7}$ **d)** $\frac{1}{2}$ **e)** $\frac{2}{3}$

4 **a)** 15%   **b)** 50%   **c)** 97%   **d)** 100%

5 **a)** £80   **b)** $5,800   **c)** €150,000   **d)** €20,000

B **Try and answer these questions.**

1 What is the population of your   **a)** country?   **b)** city?

2 How many people work for your company/study at your institution?

3 What is the average salary in your country?

4 What is the inflation rate?

5 Roughly how many people are unemployed?

6 What is the interest rate for savings?

C 🎧 **11.6 Listen to the following extracts from a radio business news programme. Underline the numbers you hear.**

1 **a)** Inflation rate: 2.0% / <u>1.2 %</u>
   b) Unemployment: 1,258,000 / 1,800,000

2 **a)** Profits increase: $1.8 billion / $1.8 million
   b) Sales increase: 80% / 18%

3 **a)** Job losses: $\frac{1}{3}$ / $\frac{1}{4}$
   b) Workforce reduction: 15,000 / 5,000

4 **a)** Interest rate reduction: 0.5% / 1.5%
   b) Economic growth: 2.8% / 1.8%

Useful language

Saying large numbers
For example, 912,757,250 =

912,	757,	250
nine hundred and twelve million,	seven hundred and fifty-seven thousand,	two hundred and fifty

British and American English differences

320 = three hundred $\begin{cases} and \text{ twenty (BrE)} \\ \text{twenty (AmE)} \end{cases}$

0 = nought / oh (BrE)   0 = zero (AmE)

Decimals
1.25   = one point two five
0.754 = nought point seven five four (BrE)
        zero point seven five four (AmE)
        point seven five four (BrE/AmE)

Fractions
$\frac{5}{7}$ = five-sevenths $\frac{1}{2}$ = a half
$\frac{2}{5}$ = two-fifths $\frac{1}{4}$ = a quarter

Percentages
65% = sixty-five percent

Currencies
£3,000,000 = three million pounds
€16,000 = sixteen thousand euros

D **You work for a marketing department which is launching a new range of mobile phones in an overseas market. You are gathering statistical information.**
Work in pairs. Student A: turn to page 140. Student B: turn to page 142.

1 Ask each other questions to complete your charts.

2 Discuss which are the best markets to launch the new range of phones in.

CASE STUDY

MARCIA LEE JEANS

Background

Marcia Lee Jeans is based in New York. Its brand is well known in the United States. The jeans sell in the upper price ranges and appeal to fashion conscious people aged 15 to 40. They are distributed in major department stores throughout the country. At present, the jeans are made in the US by a number of factories on the East coast, none of which are owned by Marcia Lee Jeans. Competition in this segment of the market is strong, so the company has to keep costs as low as possible in order to remain profitable.

In the next 10 years, Marcia Lee plans to expand in Europe and Southeast Asia so that it becomes a global company. To do this, it has decided to build its own factory in an overseas country. The factory will have approximately 2,000 workers who will produce the jeans. These workers will be recruited locally. Denim, the raw material which is used to make the jeans, will be imported from several countries.

The company is considering four countries as a location for the factory. There is some information about each country on page 105. They are code named A, B, C and D.

Task

You are members of the planning committee which must choose a location for the new factory.

1 Work individually. Study the four countries and rank them in order of suitability as a location.
2 Work in small groups. Discuss the advantages and disadvantages of each location.
3 Meet as one group, with one of you leading the discussion. Decide which is the most suitable location for the new jeans factory.

Writing

Write a letter to the head of the chamber of commerce of the country you have chosen. In the letter you should introduce Marcia Lee Jeans and suggest a possible meeting in order to discuss the proposal further.

➡ *Writing file page 130*

COUNTRY A

Economy
- Growth rate: 2% per year
- Inflation rate: 5%
- Interest rates: 10%–15%
- Unemployment rate: 25%–30%
- The country has a lot of debt and is trying to modernise its economy.

Transport
- Good rail network but poor roads
- New international airport
- The main seaport is in poor condition.

Labour
- Unskilled labour available. A lot of training needed for jeans production
- No unions in most industries
- Wage rates: very low

Comments
The country has a military government. Bribery is common. Political problems: the people in the north want to become an independent state. The government will contribute 30% towards the cost of a new factory.

COUNTRY B

Economy
- Growth rate: 1.5%
- Inflation rate: 0.5%
- Interest rates: 8%–10%
- Unemployment rate: 3%
- A modern industrial country with many manufacturing industries

Transport
- Has a fully integrated road and rail network
- International airport
- No seaport

Labour
- Not a lot of skilled labour available
- Strong unions
- Wage rates: high

Comments
The country has a stable government. It is a member of a large trading group. There are strict new laws on pollution. There are no tax incentives for building new factories. Business tax is very high.

COUNTRY C

Economy
- Growth rate: 8%
- Inflation rate: 10%
- Interest rates: 4%–6%
- Unemployment rate: 12%
- Currency exchange rate: unstable

Transport
- Good transport around the main seaports
- Small but well-managed airport
- Road network needs investment

Labour
- Not much skilled labour available
- Very strong unions in the clothing industry
- Wage rates: low but rising fast

Comments
The first free elections for a democratic government were held last year. There are limits on the profits which companies can take out of the country. Not much paperwork required for importing and exporting goods. There is a strong protest movement against international companies, which are accused of harming local firms.

COUNTRY D

Economy
- Growth rate: 4%
- Inflation rate: 5%
- Interest rates: 8%–12%
- Unemployment rate: 12%
- Government encourages the privatisation of industry

Transport
- Road and rail network is in poor condition
- Government has started a big investment programme for the transport system. It will take 5–10 years to complete.

Labour
- Large supply of skilled workers, but they are not used to working long hours
- Strong unions
- Wage rates: low

Comments
A lot of paperwork is required for new businesses. There are problems with air and water pollution. Profits are tax free for the first three years after a factory has been built. Companies must pay 5% of their profits into a fund for training their workers.

Products

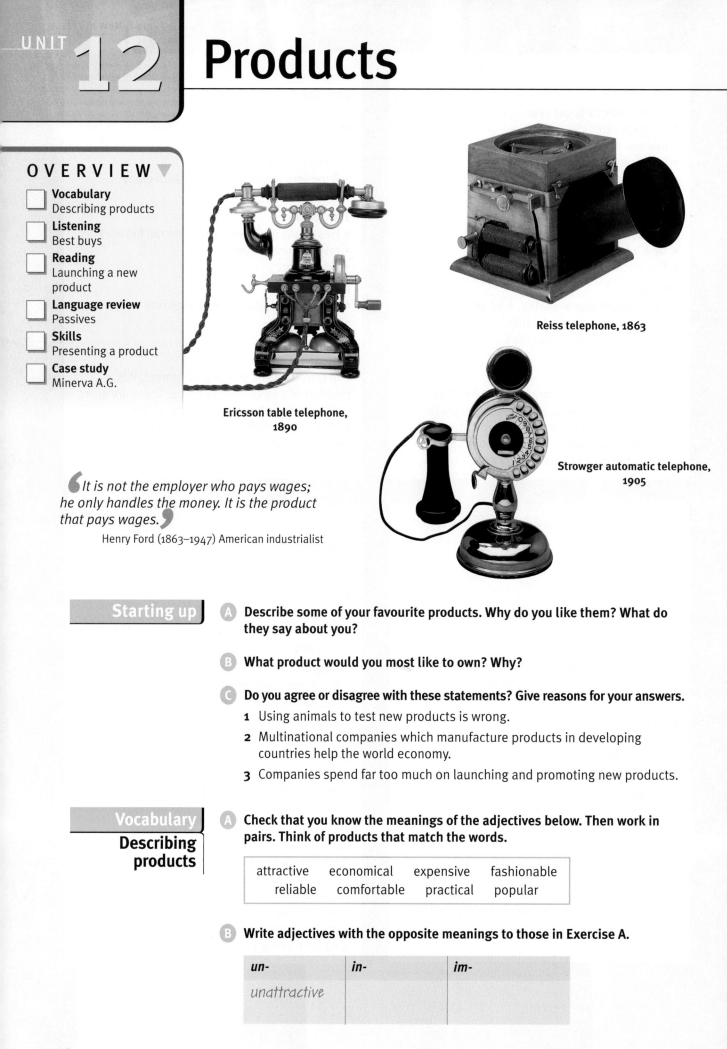

Reiss telephone, 1863

Ericsson table telephone, 1890

Strowger automatic telephone, 1905

❝*It is not the employer who pays wages; he only handles the money. It is the product that pays wages.*❞

Henry Ford (1863–1947) American industrialist

Starting up

A Describe some of your favourite products. Why do you like them? What do they say about you?

B What product would you most like to own? Why?

C Do you agree or disagree with these statements? Give reasons for your answers.

1 Using animals to test new products is wrong.

2 Multinational companies which manufacture products in developing countries help the world economy.

3 Companies spend far too much on launching and promoting new products.

Vocabulary

Describing products

A Check that you know the meanings of the adjectives below. Then work in pairs. Think of products that match the words.

attractive	economical	expensive	fashionable
reliable	comfortable	practical	popular

B Write adjectives with the opposite meanings to those in Exercise A.

un-	in-	im-
unattractive		

Black Post Office telephone, 1938

Vodafone transportable mobile telephone, 1985

Post Office telephone, 1958

Nokia mobile telephone, 2002

C **Complete these sentences with the words from the box.**

well	~~high~~	best	long	hard	high

1 IBM manufactures ....*high*...... -*tech* computer products.
2 Timberland makes a range of ....-*wearing* footwear.
3 Ferrari produces .... -*quality* sports cars.
4 Coca-Cola and Pepsico both developed ....-*selling* soft drinks.
5 Duracell sells .... -*lasting* alkaline batteries.
6 Levi jeans are a ....-*made* clothing product.

D **Use the adjectives in Exercise C to describe other companies and products. For example, *Nestlé makes many of the world's best-selling food products*.**

E **Match the verbs on the left to their meanings. Then put the verbs into a logical order to show the life cycle of a new product.**

1	launch	**a)**	to stop making
2	test	**b)**	to build or make
3	promote	**c)**	to introduce to the market
4	manufacture	**d)**	to change in order to improve
5	modify	**e)**	to try something in order to see how it works
6	discontinue	**f)**	to make a plan or drawing
7	design	**g)**	to increase sales by advertising, etc.
8	distribute	**h)**	to supply to shops, companies, customers

Listening
Best buys

A 🎧 **12.1** **Five people were asked the question, 'What is the best thing you have ever bought?' Listen and write down the thing that each person mentions.**

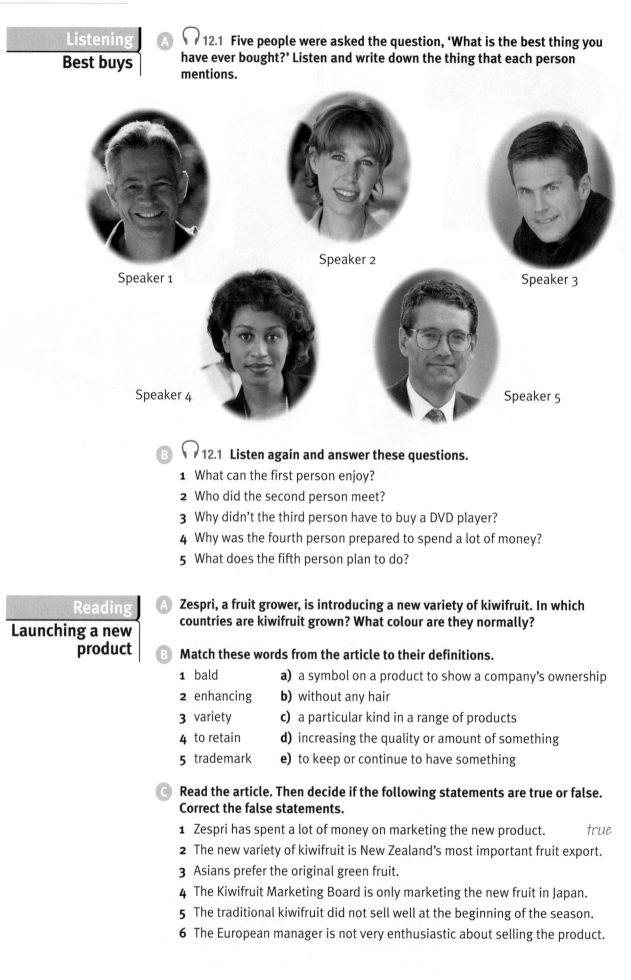

Speaker 1

Speaker 2

Speaker 3

Speaker 4

Speaker 5

B 🎧 **12.1** **Listen again and answer these questions.**

1 What can the first person enjoy?
2 Who did the second person meet?
3 Why didn't the third person have to buy a DVD player?
4 Why was the fourth person prepared to spend a lot of money?
5 What does the fifth person plan to do?

Reading
Launching a new product

A **Zespri, a fruit grower, is introducing a new variety of kiwifruit. In which countries are kiwifruit grown? What colour are they normally?**

B **Match these words from the article to their definitions.**

1 bald   **a)** a symbol on a product to show a company's ownership
2 enhancing   **b)** without any hair
3 variety   **c)** a particular kind in a range of products
4 to retain   **d)** increasing the quality or amount of something
5 trademark   **e)** to keep or continue to have something

C **Read the article. Then decide if the following statements are true or false. Correct the false statements.**

1 Zespri has spent a lot of money on marketing the new product.   *true*
2 The new variety of kiwifruit is New Zealand's most important fruit export.
3 Asians prefer the original green fruit.
4 The Kiwifruit Marketing Board is only marketing the new fruit in Japan.
5 The traditional kiwifruit did not sell well at the beginning of the season.
6 The European manager is not very enthusiastic about selling the product.

Kiwifruit growers hope to strike gold with new product

By Terry Hall

Zespri is risking millions of dollars on the launch of an entirely new product – the bald, gold kiwifruit. The effort, Zespri says, has been a great success. But with Zespri Gold making up only 10 percent of total New Zealand kiwifruit production, the company must be careful to continue to promote the traditional hairy green variety, which has annual sales of NZ$500m (US$224m) and is New Zealand's single most important fruit export.

In Japan Zespri managers decided to emphasise the fruit's health-giving, energy-enhancing qualities. The new variety is sweeter and more attractive to Asian tastes. Yu Jan Chen, regional manager for Zespri in Japan and Asia, says: 'It is ideal for the Asian markets.' He says it is selling 'very well' in Japan, and is also being marketed in South Korea and Taiwan. The export season began slowly because the traditional green fruit was unusually small and difficult to sell. However, sales picked up when the gold fruit became available.

The successful launch of the gold fruit is expected to increase profits in the long term. The Kiwifruit Marketing Board has retained all marketing and selling rights for Europe and overseas for the trademarked variety. This will protect revenue as the gold variety is planted worldwide.

The board has already signed contracts with the four largest kiwifruit co-operatives in Italy, and planting has begun. The area for planting is expected to grow steadily, eventually producing millions of trays.

As Guus Van Der Kleij, regional manager for Europe, says, 'It is an excellent product: after 25 years selling traditional green kiwifruit, you don't know how exciting it is to sell something different.'

From the *Financial Times*

FINANCIAL TIMES
World business newspaper.

D **Find words or phrases in the text which mean the following:**

1 introduction (paragraph 1)   *launch*

2 to try hard to sell a product by advertising or other activities (paragraph 1)

3 each year (paragraph 1)

4 to say that something is particularly important (paragraph 2)

5 person in charge of a particular area (paragraph 2)

6 improved (paragraph 2)

7 money received from selling goods (paragraph 3)

8 firms that are owned and run by all the employees (paragraph 4)

E **Answer these questions.**

1 What are the most important qualities of the new kiwifruit?

2 What methods can companies use to promote new food products?

3 The article says '... sales picked up when the gold fruit became available'. At what time of the year do sales of the following pick up in your country?
a) toys   **b)** ice cream   **c)** cars   **d)** greeting cards

F **Work in pairs or small groups. Brainstorm ideas for marketing the new kiwifruit in your country. Then design a one-page newspaper advertisement for Zespri Gold.**

Language review

Passives

- We make passive verb forms with the verb *to be* + past participle.
  *Zespri Gold **is marketed** in South Korea and Taiwan.*
- We often choose a passive structure when we are not interested in or it is not necessary to know who performs an action.
  *Kiwifruit **are grown** in New Zealand.*
- If we want to mention who performs an action, we can use *by*.
  *All selling rights have been retained **by** the Kiwifruit Marketing Board.*
- We can use the passive to describe a process, system or procedure.
  *At the final stage of the process, the kiwifruit **are packed** into containers.*

page 129

A Use the table below to make passive sentences. For example, *Diamonds are mined in South Africa*. Then make similar sentences about products from your own country.

Diamonds Microchips	produce	Poland Kuwait Japan
Semiconductors	manufacture	The United States
Electronic goods Coffee	make	Finland Switzerland
Leather goods Oil Rice	refine	Malaysia Brazil
Watches Coal Copper	grow	Spain South Africa
Mobile phones	mine	Zambia China

B Change these active sentences into the passive so that they sound more natural. For example, *The gold variety of the kiwifruit is planted worldwide.*

1 Workers plant the gold variety of the kiwifruit worldwide.

2 Workers in France make these Renault cars.

3 Farmers grow this rice in India.

4 The employers asked the staff for their opinions.

5 A mechanic is repairing my car at the moment.

6 Somebody has found the missing file.

7 Somebody made this toy in Japan.

C The article below describes how a health care company develops new products. Complete the article with passive forms of the verbs in brackets.

The idea for how our company's new products *are developed*.¹ (develop) is not new – it ....² (model) on the well-known example of the Body Shop.

When a new product ....³ (plan), the first step is to send Product Development Agents to the region of the developing world chosen for the project. They start by finding materials that ....⁴ (use) in the product. Then links ....⁵ (arrange) with local suppliers.

Wherever possible, products ....⁶ (manufacture) locally as well, although the finished product ....⁷ (export) for sale mostly in the developed world. Normally, products ....⁸ (ship) in large containers and ....⁹ (package) in their final form only when they reach their destination.

The Product Development Agent identifies and establishes links with local material suppliers. After that he or she ensures that these links ....¹⁰ (maintain). The agent is also responsible for producing the goods safely so that human rights ....¹¹ (respect) and local workers ....¹² (not exploit).

Skills
Presenting a product

A 🎧 **12.2 Listen to a sales manager presenting a product to some buyers. Which of the adjectives below does she use?**

> attractive ✓   fashionable   stylish   robust   elegant   user-friendly
> high-quality   well-designed   reliable   flexible   popular   practical

B 🎧 **12.2 Listen again to the presentation. How does the sales manager describe the product? Fill in the missing words and phrases.**

1. As you can see, it's .*attractive*. and ....
2. The tower .... of wood.
3. Let me .... its dimensions.
4. It .... in three colours.
5. Its .... is just under £25.
6. It's .... for storing CDs and CD-Roms.
7. It has several .... which should appeal to our customers.
8. .... is that it's easy to select the CD you want.
9. The tower is well-designed. It's ...., ... and user-friendly.
10. It really does .... of music lovers.

C **Work in small groups. Choose one of the products shown. Then turn to its Information file on page 141. Prepare a short presentation about your product. Invent any additional information that you wish.**

Then form new groups and present your products to each other. Answer any questions that you are asked about them.

Outdoor heater

Leather attaché case

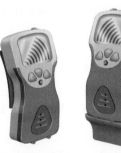

Juice extractor

Baby monitor

Useful language

Introducing the product
This is our new product.
I'm going to tell you about our new product.

Describing the product
Let me tell you about its special features.
It's made of leather/wood/steel/aluminium.
It weighs just 2.3 kilos.
It comes in a wide range of colours.

Stating the product's uses
It's ideal for travelling.
It's designed to be used with any type of material.

Mentioning selling points
It has several special features.
A very useful feature is the energy-saving design.
Another advantage is its very small size.

Inviting questions
Does anyone have any questions?
Would anyone like to ask a question?

Background

Minerva A.G., based in Munich, Germany, is a chain store which sells a range of stylish, innovative products. Many of its products feature new technology, but the stores sell everything from furniture and fashionable clothes to kitchenware and household goods. It is well-known for its original designs and high quality. On the window of every store are the words *Creativity, Imagination, Style, Novelty, Originality*.

Customer satisfaction survey

Minerva A.G. sent questionnaires to all its customers. Here is an extract from the Marketing Department's report.

> **3   Our customers say:**
>
> 3.1   Minerva A.G. has very few 'great new products' for customers with busy lifestyles.
>
> 3.2   The range of products is not as wide as it used to be.
>
> 3.3   There are too many high-tech products. Customers want fewer products but more original ones.
>
> 3.4   Most products are over €100. Customers who are looking for gifts think they are too expensive.
>
> 3.5   There are not enough special offers to encourage customers to spend more.

Need for new products

Chairperson Ulrika Nielsen and her directors have invited several foreign firms to present their new products to the Minerva A.G. board. All the companies are well-known for their innovation. The directors will choose the best and most exciting products for Minerva A.G.'s stores.

COMPANY A

Weight Monitor

Special features:
- Measures how much body fat you have
- An LCD display shows changes in your weight
- Easy-to-read graphs and charts
- Holds health and weight records for up to five years
- Price: €45

COMPANY C

Virtual Passenger

Special features:
- Chats, tells jokes, plays music, asks questions
- Keeps you awake
- Stops boredom
- 20,000 word memory – knows your interests
- Automatically opens windows
- Alarm function if driver falls asleep
- Ideal for sales reps
- Price: €500

COMPANY B

Personal Satellite Navigation System

Special features:
- Pocket-sized
- Download any world city map from your computer
- No need to carry a street map ever again
- Includes tourist information
- Slim, lightweight
- Colours: silver or black
- Price: €320

COMPANY D

Floating Globe

Special features:
- Appears to float in the air because it is controlled by magnets
- Rotates
- Lights up
- Many physical features highlighted, for example mountain ranges
- Ideal for the home or office
- Price: €220

Task

1 Work in small groups. Choose one of the companies above and prepare a presentation on its product. (Or, if you prefer, think of another product which the company is about to launch.) Invent any information you wish.

2 Form new groups and present your products. Try to persuade the Minerva A.G. directors to buy large quantities. When you are not presenting, play the role of a Minerva A.G. director and ask questions about the products.

3 After all the presentations, discuss which product is the most exciting and innovative.

Writing

As a Minerva A.G. director, write a short report on one of the products which you saw presented. Recommend whether Minerva A.G. should place a large order for the product or not.

Writing file page 135

10 Conflict

Qualities

Complete the crossword.

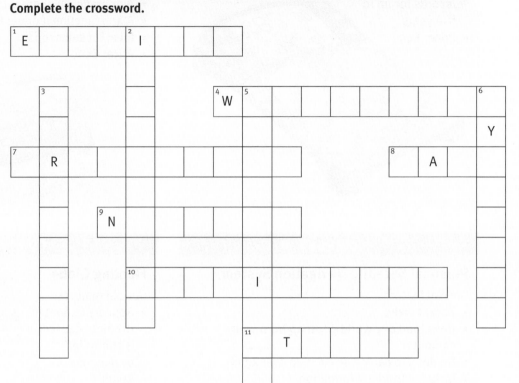

Across

1 Feelings such as anger, happiness, sadness (8)

4 Things that make you more likely to fail (10)

7 The ability to have a lot of new ideas (10)

8 When you keep cool in a difficult situation (4)

9 When you feel worried and uncomfortable (7)

10 Always doing the same thing (11)

11 Powerful (6)

Down

2 When you do not want to wait for something to happen (10)

3 When things are done according to strict rules (9)

5 A feeling of excitement and interest in what you are doing (10)

6 When someone is in a bad situation and you do or say something to help them (8)

Reading

Correct this e-mail from a friend who works in another company.

In most of the lines 1 to 5 there is one extra word that does not fit. One or two of the lines, however, are correct. If a line is correct, put a tick in the space next to that line. If there is one extra word in the line, write that word in the space.

I need to write to you because I'm feeling terrible – I don't know how much longer I can stay in this job. I told you about my colleague Keith. It's getting worse. He

1 always gets to work late and leaves off early. He never   1............
2 seems to do anything. In meetings, he are always   2............
3 interrupts people when they are talking – the only   3............
4 opinion that he's interested of in is his own. I know that   4............
5 the lots of other people in the department hate him, too.   5............

But I don't think our department manager, Lionel, knows about the problem – Lionel is very weak and even if he knew, I don't think he would do anything. And, anyway, I don't want to 'tell stories' about a colleague. What would you do in my situation? Should I try to talk to the people I work with about Keith? Perhaps we can find a way of persuading him to change his behaviour. I'd be very grateful for any advice you could give me.

Yours,

Jessica

Writing **Write an e-mail (85 to 100 words) to your friend Jessica, advising her what to do.**

11 New business

Economic terms **Complete this text with the correct alternatives.**

The economy is very unstable. By letting monetary policy run out of control, the government caused inflation to rise at one point to 20 percent. The inflation ....[1] is now down to 'only' 8 percent. However, in the last six months there has been a severe worsening in the ....[2] rate against the dollar. Total output, or ....[3], has fallen by 5 percent over the past year. Exports are declining and the ....[4] of trade is disastrous: we are importing much more than we are exporting.

The ....[5] rate, with 30 percent of people out of work, is one of the highest in the industrialised world. In order to stimulate the economy and attract foreign ....[6] the government is offering new tax ....[7] as well as making a renewed effort to reduce government ....[8]. But we need to improve education and improve the skills of our labour ....[9] in order to offer attractive investment ....[10] over the long term.

1 a) speed	**b)** height	**c)** rate
2 a) change	**b)** exchange	**c)** swap
3 a) GDP	**b)** GOP	**c)** GAR
4 a) equilibrium	**b)** balance	**c)** swing
5 a) labour	**b)** work	**c)** unemployment
6 a) investment	**b)** spending	**c)** input
7 a) excitement	**b)** incentives	**c)** inspiration
8 a) bureaucracy	**b)** bureau de change	**c)** office work
9 a) team	**b)** group	**c)** force
10 a) occasions	**b)** chances	**c)** opportunities

Time clauses

Which one of the alternatives is logically *not* possible for each sentence?

1 .... *c* .... she gets here, show her into my office.
   a) When   **b)** As soon as   **c)** Until

2 Could you take care of this problem .... I'm away?
   a) before   **b)** when   **c)** while

3 Don't do anything .... we've spoken to the people in New York.
   a) until   **b)** as soon as   **c)** before

4 I'm getting the train to Hamburg tomorrow afternoon – I'll phone you ....
   I arrive at my hotel.
   a) before   **b)** when   **c)** until

5 Please let me know .... you hear something.
   a) when   **b)** before   **c)** as soon as

6 Please hand in your visitor's badge .... you leave.
   a) until   **b)** as soon as   **c)** when

7 Do not open the door .... the train comes to a complete stop.
   a) before   **b)** until   **c)** as soon as

Writing

You work for the Euphoria Development Agency. Write a report about the economy of Euphoria for the head of Teknos, a company that is considering investing in a high-tech factory in Euphoria to make computer chips.

Summarise the information below in 100 to 120 words, and recommend at the end of it that Teknos should make this investment.

Euphoria: key facts

Economy	Labour
• Growth rate: 7% per year • Inflation rate: 2% per year • Unemployment rate: 2% at present	• Education system excellent: a lot of skilled labour at every level – workers and managers
Transport and infrastructure	**Comments**
• Heavy traffic on roads causing slow journeys and distribution problems, but very fast rail services	• Some commentators talk about 'laziness' of young people who have too much money to spend

12 Products

Compounds

Complete each of these sentences by using a compound starting with the word in brackets, and using one of the words a) to f). Each word is used once.

a) wearing   **c)** tech   **e)** selling
b) quality   **d)** lasting   **f)** made

1 Go to Saveaway Supermarkets for (high-) .... meat produced with the best farming methods.

2 *Valley of the Dolls* by Jacqueline Susann has sold 30 million copies – it's the (best-) .... novel of all time.

3 Doc Martens boots – average life seven years – are (long-) .... footwear.

4 Buy Good Era tyres – they're so (hard-) .... : 200,000 kilometres and they still look the same.

5 German cars are famous for being solid and (well-) ....

6 No more posting of documents from one department to another – Docushare is the (high-) .... solution to distributing information on the Internet.

Reading

Read this report by an expert on products. In each line 1 to 5 there is one wrong word. Underline the wrong word and write the correct word in the space provided.

Can we have too many products?

There are two cars in the garage. In the living room, there is a wide-screen television with 100 channels, and first-class hi-fi equipment. Each child has a television in his or her

1 bedroom. The kitchen contain a dishwasher, an ordinary oven ....

2 and a microwave oven. The cupboard in the bedroom is fill of ....

3 designer-label clothes. Is it possible too have so many products ....

4 that we don't need any more? Some economy think so. They ....

5 points to Japan, where demand for certain goods has been flat ....

for 10 years now. They say that one reason for this is that Japanese people have all the material goods they want and save their money instead of buying more. Compare this with the poorest countries in the world, where there is one television set for every 60 people.

Writing

Look at the products in the case study on page 113. In the end, Minerva A.G. developed all of these products and you bought ONE of them. Write one of these letters (90 to 110 words) to Minerva A.G.

1 Thank them. Tell Minerva
   - which product you bought
   - why you bought the product
   - how you have used it
   - why you like it
   - whether you think it offers good value for money
   - whether you will buy another one – if so, ask them to send you details of future models

2 Criticise the product. Tell Minerva
   - which product you bought
   - why you bought the product
   - how you have used it
   - why you don't like it
   - that you would like a refund

Grammar reference

1 Modals 1: *can/could/would*

Form

+ I/You/He/She/It/We/They **can** go.
− I/You/He/She/It/We/They **can't** (= **cannot**) go.
? **Can** I/you/he/she/it/we/they/go?

Uses

1 We use *can* and *could* to:

- make requests.

  Can *I make a phone call?*
  Could *you tell me the time, please?* (a little more formal)

- give or refuse permission.

  *You **can** use my mobile phone.*
  *You **can't** go in there. It's private.*

- make an offer.

  Can *I take your coat?*
  *I **can** take you to the station if you like.*

- describe ability.

  *Women **can** become train drivers.*
  *When he was younger he **could** (= was able to) run a marathon in under three hours.*

- say that something is possible or impossible.

  *You **can** make a lot of money if you work hard.*
  *I **can't** get through to them. Their phone's always engaged.*

2 We also use *could* to refer to future possibilities.

  *I think we **could** increase our market share in the long term.*

3 We use *would* to:

- make requests.

  Would *you open the door for me, please?*

- make offers.

  Would *you like a glass of water?*

- describe imaginary situations.

  *I **would** buy a Ferrari if I had enough money.*

2   Modals 2: necessity and obligation: *must, need to, have to, should*

1   We often use *must, need to* and *has/have to* to say that something is compulsory or necessary.

    *We **must** be patient when our goals are for the long term.*
    *Companies **have to** advertise to let consumers know they exist.*
    *I **need to** have the figures before next Monday's meeting.*

2   *Need* can also have a passive meaning.

    *The report **needs** to be checked before the end of the week.*

3   We use *had to* to refer to a past obligation.

    *When I lived in Tokyo I **had to** learn Japanese.*

4   We use *should* and *shouldn't* to give advice or to suggest the right course of action.

    *A CV **should** be printed on good quality notepaper.*
    *It **shouldn't** be more than two pages long.*

•   *Should* often follows the verbs *suggest* and *think*.

    *I suggest/think we **should** aim at the top end of the market.*

5   We use *should* to say that something is likely in the future.

    *Interest rates **should** come down soon – that's what the economists are predicting.*

6   We use *don't have to* and *don't need to* when there is no obligation.

    *You **don't have to** queue up when you buy online.*
    *If you buy now, you **don't need to** pay anything until next year.*

7   We use *must not* when things are forbidden or against the law.

    *Drivers **must not** park their vehicles by a traffic light.*

•   Compare the uses of *must not* and *don't have to* in the sentence below.

    *In many companies employees **must not** wear jeans, but they **do not have to** wear a formal suit and tie.*

3 Present simple and present continuous

Present simple

Form

+ I/You/We/They **work**.
  He/She/It **works**.

− I/You/We/They **don't work**.
  He/She/It **doesn't work**.

? **Do** I/you/we/they **work**?
  Does he/she/it **work**?

Uses

1 We use the present simple to:

- give factual information about permanent activities.
  *Valentino **makes** luxury chocolates.*

- describe a state that doesn't change.
  *He **looks** like his father.*
  *Nothing **succeeds** like success.*

- talk about routine activities, repeated actions or habits.

2 This use of the present simple is associated with adverbs of frequency.

  *We usually **have** our weekly sales meeting on Mondays.*
  *I often **travel** abroad on business.*
  *We sometimes **get** complaints, but not many.*

3 Verbs that describe permanent states or situations are used in the present simple, not with *-ing*.

  *What do you **mean**?* (NOT *What are you meaning?)
  *The decision **involves** taking a risk.* (NOT *The decision is involving ...)
  *The premises **don't belong** to them.* (NOT *The premises aren't belonging ...)
  *He **doesn't remember** her name.* (NOT *He isn't remembering ...)

Present continuous

Form

+ I **am going**.
  He/She/It **is going**.
  You/We/They **are going**.

− I **am not going**.
  He/She/It **is not going**.
  You/We/They **are not going**.

? **Am** I **going**?
  Is he/she/it **going**?
  Are you/we/they **going**?

Uses

We use the present continuous to:

- describe activities in progress at the moment of speaking.
  *She**'s talking** to him on the phone right now.*

- describe temporary situations.
  *The delegation **is staying** at the Hilton until Friday.*

- refer to future arrangements.
  *He**'s starting** a new job next week.*

- describe changing situations.
  *We**'re developing** a new marketing strategy.*

4 Past simple and past continuous

Past simple

Form

+ I/You/We/They **worked**.
  He/She/It **worked**.

– I/You/He/She/It/We/They **didn't work**.

? **Did** I/you/he/she/it/we/they **work**?

Uses

1 We use the past simple to refer to states and actions which finished in the past.

   *He **left** for Australia yesterday.*
   *When I was young, I **wanted** to be a pilot.*

2 The action can be short, long or repeated.

   *They **took** a taxi to get here.*
   *The flight **lasted** 10 hours.*
   *I **took** the same train every day.*

Past continuous

Form

+ I/He/She/It **was working**.
  You/We/They **were working**.

– I/He/She/It **was not working**.
  You/We/They **were not working**.

? **Was** I/he/she/it **working**?
  Were you/we/they **working**?

Uses

1 We use the past continuous to:

• talk about actions that were not yet finished and continued over a period of time.

   *At that time, we **were** still **trying** to solve our recruitment problem.*

   Sometimes this period of time includes another event which is completed.

   *She **had** an accident while she **was driving** to work.*
   *I **was talking** to him on the phone when I **heard** an explosion.*

• refer to situations that were changing over time in the past.

   *During the 1980s many of the older industries **were closing** down.*
   *At that time we **were coming** out of recession and things **were improving**.*

2 We do not use the past continuous with verbs that describe opinions and thoughts.

   *What **did** you **think** of her proposal?* (NOT *were you thinking)
   *What exactly **did** she **mean**?* (NOT *was she meaning)
   *He **didn't know** that I **knew** what he was doing.* (NOT *wasn't knowing that I was knowing)

5 | Past simple and present perfect

Present perfect

Form

+ I/You/We/They **have worked**.
  He/She/It **has worked**.

– I/You/He/She/It/We/They **haven't worked**.

? **Have** I/you/we/they **worked**?
  Has he/she/it **worked**?

Uses

1 We use the present perfect to:

- talk about actions that continue from the past to the present.

  We **have been** in this business for over 50 years.
     (= We are still in business.)

- talk about past events that have an impact in the present.

  Recently profits **have fallen** sharply because of strong competition.
  Genova **has had** to cut costs by reorganising the workforce.

- talk about life experiences.

  He**'s worked** in a number of different firms.
  I**'ve been** to London on many occasions.
  She**'s** never **had to** lead a team before. (= in her life up to now)

2 Because the time reference includes the present, we use time expressions
  that refer to both present and past.

  So far, we **have captured** 30% of the market.
  This week, I**'ve written** three long reports.
  Over the last few days, I **have had** too much work to do.

Present perfect versus past simple

1 We use the past simple for completed actions that happened in the past.
  Capricorn **opened** its first store in 1984.

2 Because the time reference is past, we use time expressions that refer to
  finished past time.

  Last year we **increased** turnover by 15%.
  Five years ago, we **didn't have** an overseas subsidiary.
  She **joined** the company **three months ago**.

3 The decision to use the past simple or present perfect depends on how we
  see the event. If we see it as related to the present, we use the present
  perfect. If we see it as completed and in the past, we use the past simple.

  I**'ve known** Bill for many years.
     (= We are still in touch.)

  I **knew** Bill when I was at college.
     (= We don't keep in touch.)

6 Multi-word verbs

1 A multi-word verb is a combination of a verb and one or two particles (like *at, away, down, in, on, up*).

2 Types of multi-word verbs

- without an object
  *The photocopier has **broken down**.*
  *Something has **come up**.* (= happened)

- with an object – separable
  The direct object can come after the verb and before the particle.

  *Could you **turn on** the coffee machine?/Could you **turn** the coffee machine **on**?*

- with an object – inseparable
  *The director cannot **do without** his secretary.* (NOT *The director cannot do his secretary without.*)

3 In many cases the phrasal verb is more informal than its synonym.

  *How did you **find out**?* (= discover the information)
  *We **set off** early.* (= departed)

4 Many phrasal verbs are idiomatic; in other words, their meaning is difficult to interpret. However, it can help if you understand the meanings of the particles. For example:

- ***away*** (creating distance)
  *I'm **going away** next week.*
  *Don't **run away**. I need to talk to you.*

- ***on*** (continuing)
  ***Carry on** the good work!*
  *The meeting **went on** until seven o'clock.*

- ***over*** (considering)
  *I need time to **think** it **over**.*
  *Come and see me, and we'll **talk** it **over**.*

- ***up*** (completing)
  *Some urgent matters need **clearing up**.*
  ***Drink up**. We've got to go.*

  (For further information, consult the *Longman Dictionary of Phrasal Verbs*.)

7 | Questions

Yes–No questions

In questions that can be answered with either *yes* or *no*, we put an auxiliary verb before the subject.

Are you coming?	Yes, I am./No, I'm not.
Can you drive a truck?	Yes, I can./No, I can't.
Do you know his name?	Yes, I do./No, I don't.
Did you arrive on time?	Yes, I did./No, I didn't.
Have you heard the news?	Yes, I have./No, I haven't.
Will you have time?	Yes, I will./No, I won't.

Open questions

1 We use question words such as *what, who, where, when, why* and *how* to ask for more information. The question word comes before the auxiliary verb.

To ask about	We use
A thing	**What** is the brand name?
	Which door is it?
A person	**Who** is the Chief Executive?
A place	**Where** do you come from?
A reason	**Why** are you putting up your prices?
A moment in time	**What time** did the meeting start?
	When did the goods arrive?
A period of time	**How long** did you stay in Beijing?
The number of times	**How many times** have you been to China?
Quantity (with plural nouns)	**How many** cases did you order?
Quantity (with uncountable nouns)	**How much** money do you have on you?
The way you do something	**How** do you manage to read so quickly?

2 We use *what* if there are many possible answers and *which* if there are fewer possible answers.

What is their policy?
Which of these cases is yours?

3 If *who* or *what* is the subject of the sentence, the word order is the same as in a statement.

Who looks after the travel arrangements?
What happens when things go wrong?

4 If *who, what* or *which* asks about the object, the verb comes before the subject.

Who shall I get in touch with?
What number did you ring?
Which restaurant have you chosen?

5 The question word *how* can be followed by an adjective or adverb.

How big is the warehouse?
How good is your Spanish?
How well do you speak Spanish?
How far is the hotel from here?
How often do you travel abroad?

8 Future plans

1 We use the present continuous for future arrangements.

   *What **are** you **doing** next weekend?*
   *We**'re visiting** our suppliers next week.*

2 We also use *going to* for arrangements, plans and intentions.

   *What **are** you **going to** do next weekend?*
   *We**'re going to** visit our suppliers next week.*
   *I**'m going to** talk to you today about my company.*

3 But we do NOT use the present continuous to make predictions for the future. Compare:

   *The transport strike **is going to cause** a real problem.*
     (= This is anticipated for the future.)
   *The transport strike **is causing** a real problem.*
     (= The strike has started and the effects are present.)

4 Some verbs like *anticipate, expect, look forward to, hope* and *plan* automatically refer to the future. These verbs can be used in either the simple or continuous form.

   *I **look forward to** seeing you soon.*
   *I **am looking forward to** seeing you soon.*
   *We **hope** to do better next year.*
   *We **are hoping** to do better next year.*
   *We **plan** to attract more foreign investment.*
   *We **are planning** to attract more foreign investment.*

Other future forms

1 *Will* is very often used for predictions.

   *The forecast says that tomorrow **will** be warm and sunny.*
   *I don't think they **will** complain.*
   *She **won't** like what you've written about her.*

2 We use the contracted form *'ll* to make spontaneous offers.

   *I**'ll** help you write the report if you like.*

9 | Reported speech

We use reporting verbs like *say, tell* and *ask* to report what other people say.

1 Reporting words just said

- In this case, the situation is still present.
*The boss **says** she **wants** to see you immediately.*

2 Reporting words said in the past

- Words that are said in one place at one particular time may be reported in another place at another time. Because of the change in time there may be a change of tense or modal auxiliary. A different pronoun is used to suit the context.

Actual words	Reported words
'We are not going to panic.'	*He said they were not going to panic.*
'I left my briefcase at work.'	*She said she (had) left her briefcase at work.*
'I've already spoken to her.'	*He said he had already spoken to her.*
'We won't know before Friday.'	*She said they wouldn't know before Friday.*
'I can't give you a lower price.'	*He said he couldn't give me a lower price.*

- *Would, could* and *should* do not change.

'I would tell you if I could.'	*She said she would tell me if she could.*
'You should be more careful.'	*He said I should be more careful.*

3 *Say* versus *tell*

- We do not usually use a person object (*me, us*, etc.) after *say*.
*She **said** she would come later.* (NOT *She said me ...*)

- But after *tell*, we indicate who receives the information.
*She **told me** she would come later.*

- We can use *that* directly after *say*, but not directly after *tell*.
*He **said that** he understood the reason.* (NOT *He told that ...*)

- *Tell* also means 'to inform' or 'to instruct'.
*He **told** me he was interested in my proposal.*
*She **told** me to hurry up.*

4 Reporting questions

- We use *ask* (with or without an object) to report questions.

- Note the word order: (1) question word (2) subject (3) verb.
*He **asked** (her) **when she wanted** to take her vacation.*
*He **asked** (her) **if/ whether she wanted** to take her vacation in July or August.*

10 Conditionals

We use *if + will/would* to talk about imaginary and hypothetical situations.

First conditional
(*if* + present simple, *will* + base form of the verb)

When bargaining we often use conditional sentences to make offers and counter-offers.

*If you **arrange** for delivery at your risk and expense, we**'ll agree** to a price of 20,000 euros.*

*If I **agree** to those conditions, I**'ll** only **be able to** offer three months' guarantee.*

Second conditional
(*if* + past simple, *would* + base form of the verb)

1 When the situation is less likely to happen or be accepted, we use the second conditional.

*If we **had** more money to spend, we **would be** interested, but we don't.*

2 Sometimes the condition is logically impossible to fulfil.

*If he was the Queen of England, he**'d sell** Buckingham Palace.*

Points to remember

1 The position of the *if* clause and the main clause can be changed.

*I would lend him some money **if** he needed it.*
If he needed it, I would lend him some money.

2 We cannot use *will* or *would* in the *if* clause.

*If I ~~will~~ go to Japan, I'll probably go to a tea ceremony.
    knew
*If I ~~would know~~ the answer I would tell you.

3 It is possible to use *If I were* rather than *If I was*, especially when giving advice.

*If I **were** the minister of finance, I'd reduce taxation.*
*If I **were** you, I'd buy those shares now.*

4 Instead of *would* we can use *might* or *could*, depending on the meaning.

*If he relaxed more, he **might** not be so stressed.*
*If he wanted to, he **could** become CEO.*

Writing file

Letters

Salutation

When you know the name of the recipient:
Dear Mr/Mrs/Ms/Miss von Trotta

Note: In AmE Mr., Mrs. and Ms. include a full stop/period, e.g. Mr. von Trotta

When you don't know the name of the recipient:
Dear Sir or Madam (BrE)
Dear Sir or Madam: (AmE)

Main point

It is a good idea to put the main point at the beginning of the letter. People read the first paragraph carefully, but not always everything else.

Use the pronoun *we* when writing for your company. This is more formal than *I*.

Endings (BrE)

When you know the name of the recipient:
Yours sincerely

When you don't know the name of the recipient:
Yours faithfully

Endings (AmE)
Yours truly,
Sincerely,

Sign the letter with both first and second names. Then print your name and position under the signature.

Common abbreviations

Re:	regarding
pp	(on behalf of) when you sign the letter for another person
Enc(s).	documents are enclosed with the letter
cc:	copies (The names of the people who receive a copy are included in the letter.)

European *Business* Associates

26 Rue de Glion
1820 Montreux
Vaud Canton

Mr Heinrich von Trotta
Schneemans AG
Hapsburger Platz 1
80333 Munich

3 May 200-

Dear Mr von Trotta

Re: Invitation to speak at next conference

On behalf of European Business Associates we would like to invite you to be a keynote speaker at our 'Responsible Technologies for the Global Economy' conference planned for 19–21 October next year.

European Business Associates is Europe's leading business-oriented media production company. We broadcast business programmes for television and radio throughout the European Union, including *Business Tod@y* every morning from 07.00 on CNM.

We would be very pleased if you would present for us at the conference. As Europe's leading manufacturer of environmentally friendly high-tech equipment, we believe you could help many other companies move in the same direction.

We hope this invitation is of interest and look forward to hearing from you.

Yours sincerely

Brigitte Sea

Ms Brigitte Sea
Events Manager

Encs.   Conference brochures
cc: Jean Thornett-Smith
        Senior Director

Memos

MEMO

To: **Charles Stancombe**
            CFO
From: **Maria Castellano**
            Human Resources
Date: **15 July 200-**
Subject: **Appointment:**
            Commercial Manager, France

I have interviewed three candidates for this position
and recommend the appointment of Tim Skooba.
My reasons are as follows:

1   He has the required qualifications.
2   He has a lot of experience with the products
        we sell in the French market.
3   He speaks French fluently.
4   His removal expenses will be minimal as he
        has no family at present.

If you approve our recommendation, I will prepare the
contract for signature. Please let me know your
decision as soon as possible.

M.C.

cc: Thierry Baptiste
        CEO

> Memos are used only inside the company.

> They should include the following headings:
> *To/From/Date/Subject.*

> They should be short and include only useful
> information.

> Points should be arranged in logical order. In
> longer memos it is normal to number the
> different points.

> Memo style is formal or neutral.

> You can end with your initials or a signature.

Notice

Drucker and Drucker SOLICITORS

STAFF NOTICE

On Thursday 29 July there will be a staff and
management meeting to discuss opening a New
York branch of the company.

We look forward to hearing your suggestions as
to how to ask for volunteers for relocation.

Joanna Grey
Office Manager
26 July 200-

> Notices are used to inform people about changes
> of plan or to give instructions or warnings.

> Notices need a clear heading.

> Information must be clear. The tone is normally
> formal.

> The name and position of the person who wrote
> the notice and the date must be included.

Faxes

Faxes have the following headings: To/From/Fax number/Date/Number of pages/Subject.

The style of the fax can be formal, as in a business letter, or informal. This depends on who you are writing to.

Points can be numbered for clarity.

Regards is often used for the ending. More formal endings (Yours sincerely/Yours faithfully) are also acceptable, if you prefer.

Fulton Chamber of Commerce

Fax Transmission

To	Thierry Baptiste, CEO	**Fax no.**	+33 769 76980
From	James Baker	**Fax no.**	+44 1858 740675
Date	5 April 200-	**Pages**	*(including this page)* 1
Subject	Your letter, 2 April 200-		

Dear Mr Baptiste

Thank you for your letter of 2 April asking about the possibility of opening a factory for the manufacture of your products in Fulton. Let me answer some of your questions.

1 Employees

Yes, Fulton has a large workforce of well-trained and hard-working possible employees available.

2 Infrastructure

Road and rail links to the main cities in the UK, the airports and the ports are excellent.

3 Local tax

In certain situations it is possible to arrange favourable tax conditions for start-up organisations.

If you would like to discuss the possibilities further, please call my office to arrange a meeting for when you visit the UK. I look forward to hearing from you.

Regards

James Baker

James Baker
Chief Development Officer

e-mails

E-mails can have a formal business style or a very informal style, similar to spoken English.

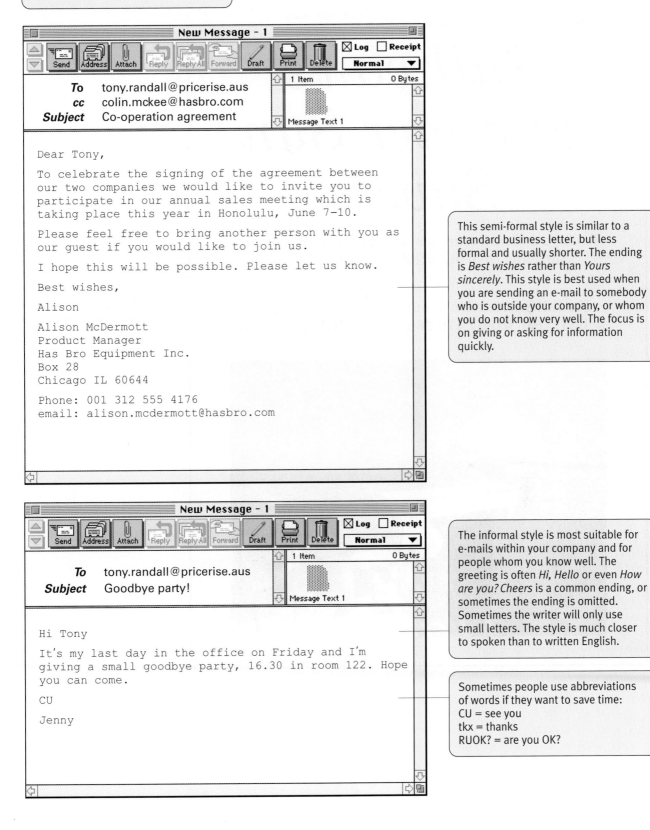

New Message - 1

Send Address Attach Reply Reply All Forward Draft Print Delete

☒ Log ☐ Receipt
Normal ▼

1 Item   0 Bytes

Message Text 1

To   tony.randall@pricerise.aus
cc   colin.mckee@hasbro.com
Subject   Co-operation agreement

Dear Tony,

To celebrate the signing of the agreement between our two companies we would like to invite you to participate in our annual sales meeting which is taking place this year in Honolulu, June 7-10.

Please feel free to bring another person with you as our guest if you would like to join us.

I hope this will be possible. Please let us know.

Best wishes,

Alison

Alison McDermott
Product Manager
Has Bro Equipment Inc.
Box 28
Chicago IL 60644

Phone: 001 312 555 4176
email: alison.mcdermott@hasbro.com

> This semi-formal style is similar to a standard business letter, but less formal and usually shorter. The ending is *Best wishes* rather than *Yours sincerely*. This style is best used when you are sending an e-mail to somebody who is outside your company, or whom you do not know very well. The focus is on giving or asking for information quickly.

New Message - 1

Send Address Attach Reply Reply All Forward Draft Print Delete

☒ Log ☐ Receipt
Normal ▼

1 Item   0 Bytes

Message Text 1

To   tony.randall@pricerise.aus
Subject   Goodbye party!

Hi Tony

It's my last day in the office on Friday and I'm giving a small goodbye party, 16.30 in room 122. Hope you can come.

CU

Jenny

> The informal style is most suitable for e-mails within your company and for people whom you know well. The greeting is often *Hi, Hello* or even *How are you? Cheers* is a common ending, or sometimes the ending is omitted. Sometimes the writer will only use small letters. The style is much closer to spoken than to written English.

> Sometimes people use abbreviations of words if they want to save time:
> CU = see you
> tkx = thanks
> RUOK? = are you OK?

133

Sales leaflets

> Sales leaflets must be clear, simple and easy to understand.

Sullivan's Summer Sun Savers

Book your Greek summer holiday before the end of April and save up to 20% on normal prices!

For full information about our range of exclusive holidays call **01807 476 666** for our **FREE** brochure.

> Provide some way for the public to contact you.

Reports

A report should be well organised with information in a logical order. There is no set layout for a report. It will depend on:
a) the type of report
b) the company style

The format used here is suitable for formal reports:
- title
- executive summary
- introduction
- findings
- conclusion
- recommendations

Business Software plc

Product report

Executive summary

We have been contacted by Lenz AG, a German manufacturer of mobile telephones, and asked about the possibility of a co-operation agreement. We would adapt our business software for use in their products. Tests show that their product is a very good one and popular with our target market.

The executive summary is a summary of the main points and conclusion of the report. It gives the reader a quick overview of the total situation.

Introduction

This report will look at:
- the hardware manufacturer and their equipment
- software that could be used on their mobile phones
- the advantages of working together
- recommendations for action

The introduction shows the points that will be looked at.

Findings

1 Lenz has been developing cheap, small-scale electronic devices for thirty-five years. In the last five years they have focussed on more expensive mobile phones for businesspeople. These have been very successful. One in four mobile phones for the business market is a Lenz.

2 Our new 'Executive Organiser' software has a lot of attractive features for the travelling businessperson (e.g. address book, e-mailware, voice recorder, street finder function, etc.)

3 Market research shows that there is a big interest in our products being used on machines apart from computers.

The findings are the facts discovered.

Conclusion

The two companies have products which fit well together.

The conclusion is what you think about the facts and how you interpret them.

Recommendation

We should have a meeting with representatives from Lenz as soon as possible to discuss a joint venture between our companies, with the aim of putting our software onto their mobile phones.

Recommendations are practical suggestions to deal with the situation and ideas for making sure future activities run more easily.

Tracy Cruickshank
Research and Development Director
19 October 200 -

1 Careers, Skills, Exercise F, page 11

Student B
1 You want to apply for the job in the advertisement. Call Lochlin Plc and ask for Laurie Thompson.
2 Some time after you call Lochlin Plc, Laurie Thompson calls you back. Ask about how you can apply for the job. You also want to know when the closing date for applications is.

**Lochlin Plc
Sales representatives**

Exciting new career opportunities for the right people.

Have you got the qualities we need?

Call Laurie Thompson on
020 7946 4021
for more information.

---

2 Selling online, Skills, Exercise E, page 19

Company manager
You want:
1 A one-year contract
   You want to see how well the company does the job and if they are reliable before giving them a long contract.
2 To have the website tested every three months
   You want the maintenance costs to be as low as possible. However, you would like to have weekly checks on the security of the website.
3 Response time – two hours
   You want to contact them at any hour by phone if there is an emergency. You want the maintenance company to solve any problems within two hours.

2 Selling online, Case study: Lifetime Holidays, page 21

Director: Lifetime Holidays
The points you need to negotiate are listed below, together with your negotiating position for each one.

Negotiating point	Your position
Length of contract	• Three years e.g. *'We need a three-year contract.'*
Destinations	• Focus only on your Mediterranean holidays
Customers	• Aim at the 30–50 age group
Car hire and insurance	• Do not offer these services at present
Advertising budget	• £100,000. Share costs on a 50/50 basis • Media: Mail shots and press advertising
Investment and profits	• 60% Lifetime Holidays/40% DirectSun (Your company is bigger and better known.)
Project management	• Suggest that your company manages the project as you have greater management experience and knowledge.

9 Managing people, Case study: The way we do things, page 85

C Sales representatives (Muller group)
You should give your opinions about the points on the agenda. Try to persuade the Sales Manager and the Deputy Sales Manager to accept your point of view, but help them to work out an action plan which will improve the effectiveness of the team.
Note: You usually meet your sales targets and often exceed them.

4 Great ideas, Skills, Exercise E, page 39

Role card A

> **Chairperson**
> You will lead the meeting. Ask for participants' opinions, encourage discussion and help them reach agreement. You must decide the following points concerning the marketing of Worldbeater.
> 1 Its selling price
> 2 Its target consumer
> 3 Special offers for first purchase
> 4 Advertising/promotion

Role card B

> **Participant**
> You have the following opinions concerning Worldbeater.
> Selling price: $240 approximately
> Target consumer: Professional players and serious club players
> Special offer for first purchase: 30 free tennis balls
> Advertising/promotion: Specialist magazines such as *Professional Tennis*

Role card C

> **Participant**
> You have the following opinions concerning Worldbeater.
> Selling price: $150
> Target consumer: All tennis players, all age groups
> Special offer for first purchase: Free tennis at a local club
> Advertising/promotion: Advertisements in national/local newspapers and television commercials

Role card D

> **Participant**
> You have the following opinions concerning Worldbeater.
> Selling price: $180
> Target consumer: All tennis players, all age groups
> Special offer for first purchase: A free T-shirt with the Freestyle logo on it
> Advertising/promotion: Advertising in clubs, at public tennis courts and in the press

Role card E

> **Participant**
> You have the following opinions concerning Worldbeater.
> Selling price: $200
> Target consumer: People with money and fashion-conscious tennis players
> Special offer for first purchase: A 20% discount off any Freestyle product
> Advertising/promotion: Endorsement contracts with famous players or film stars

10 Conflict, Case study: European Campers, page 97

> **Todd Foster**
> You want Olivier Moyon to leave the company. Try to persuade Charles Holden to let Olivier go. If Charles does not agree, try to negotiate a suitable solution to the problem.

5 Stress, Discussion, Exercise A, page 45

Actor	7.2	Hairdresser	4.3
Teacher	6.2	Banker	3.7
Bus driver	5.4	Librarian	2.0

9 Managing people, Case study: The way we do things, page 85

D   Sales representatives (Peterson group)
You should give your opinion about the points on the agenda. Try to persuade the Sales Manager and the Deputy Sales Manager to accept your point of view, but help them to work out an action plan which will improve the effectiveness of the team.
Note: You often meet your sales targets but rarely exceed them.

10 Conflict, Skills, Exercise E, page 95

Union Representative
The workers are very unhappy with the price increases. They think that the subsidised restaurant is part of their terms and conditions of work. They are also angry that management did not discuss their plans with them first. You want to negotiate a solution to the problem. Your objectives are:
1 to get subsidised meals back immediately, or
2 to postpone the cuts in subsidies until the staff have been properly consulted.

11 New business, Skills, Exercise D, page 103

Student A
Ask and answer questions to complete the information in your tables. For example, *What's the population of Tokyo? (Twenty-six point four million* OR *Twenty-six million, four hundred thousand).*

Biggest cities (population in millions)		Computers per 100 people	
1 Tokyo	....	1 Luxembourg	73.2
2 Mumbai (Bombay)	18.2	2 Singapore	45.8
3 Mexico City	....	3 United States	....
4 São Paulo	17.8	4 Switzerland	....
5 New York	16.6	5 Australia	....
6 Lagos	....	6 Denmark	37.7

Oldest populations (% aged over 65)		Cars per 1,000 people	
1 Italy	....	1 Lebanon	....
2 Greece	17.9	2= Brunei	576
3 Sweden	....	2= Luxembourg	576
4 Japan	17.1	4 Italy	....
5 Spain	17.0	5 Iceland	510
6 Belgium	....	6 Germany	....

2 Selling online, Case study: Lifetime Holidays, page 21

Director: DirectSun
The points you need to negotiate are listed below, together with your negotiating position for each one.

Negotiating point	Your position
Length of contract	• Five years e.g. *'We need a five-year contract.'*
Destinations	• Offer all the holidays in both companies' catalogues
Customers	• Aim at all age groups
Car hire and insurance	• Provide these services as they are very profitable for your company.
Advertising budget	• £300,000 – at least! Share costs on a 70%/30% basis (70% Lifetime Holidays) • Media: Include radio advertising
Investment and profits	• 50/50 basis
Project management	• Suggest that your company manages the project because of your greater experience and knowledge of selling online.

12 Products, Skills, Exercise C, page 111

Product 1: OUTDOOR HEATER
Function: To heat the air outside a building
• Gives out a lot of heat for 26 hours
• Powered by propane gas
• Easy to regulate the heat
• Light and easy to move
• Can be used in all weathers
• Easy to clean
• Attractive design
PRICE: €299

Product 2: LEATHER ATTACHÉ CASE
Function : To carry business documents
• Expandable case with desktop facility
• Twin combination locks
• 3 compartments
• 2 extra pockets
• Pen and credit card holders
• 2-year guarantee
• Dimensions: 40cm (height) 49cm (width) 15cm (depth)
PRICE: €70

Product 3: BABY MONITOR
Function : To check the health of a sleeping baby
• Works up to a 100-metre range
• Powered by mains or battery
• Low-battery indicator
• Adjustable volume
• Has a belt clip and also a stand
• Easy to use and very light
• 3-year guarantee
PRICE : €48

Product 4: JUICE EXTRACTOR
Function : To extract juice from fruit and vegetables
• Juices whole fruit and vegetables (hard and soft)
• Powerful motor
• Easy to pour juice
• Safety locking lid
• All parts easy to remove and can be washed in a dishwasher
• Stainless steel filter
• 10-year motor guarantee, 3-year parts and labour guarantee
• Free recipe book
PRICE : €68

7 Marketing, Skills, Exercise H, page 67

European Sales Manager
You want to do the following during the phone call.

1 Tell the Marketing Director when and where the focus group takes place.
Details are as follows:

Location   Commercial Institute
                5 Rue Pierre Charron
                Paris

Date/Time   Friday 29 July at 14.00

2 Note down the names of two people who the Marketing Director wishes to invite to the focus group.

3 Answer his/her questions about last month's sales results in France.
Details are as follows:

Total sales   €3.2 million
                Sales were 8% higher than the same period last year.

10 Conflict, Skills, Exercise E, page 95

General Manager
You think the staff restaurant still offers good value for money, despite the cuts in subsidies. Prices are roughly similar to those in other companies in your area. The company has to reduce costs or the staff's salaries will be affected. You want to negotiate and get a good solution to the problem. Your objectives are:
1 to listen carefully to what the union representative says.
2 to explain why the cuts in subsidies are necessary.

11 New business, Skills, Exercise D, page 103

Student B
Ask and answer questions to complete the information in your tables. For example, *What's the population of Mumbai? (Eighteen point two million* OR *Eighteen million, two hundred thousand).*

Biggest cities (population in millions)		Computers per 100 people	
1 Tokyo	26.4	1 Luxembourg	....
2 Mumbai (Bombay)	....	2 Singapore	....
3 Mexico City	18.1	3 United States	45.5
4 São Paulo	....	4 Switzerland	42.1
5 New York	....	5 Australia	41.1
6 Lagos	13.4	6 Denmark	....

Oldest populations (% aged over 65)		Cars per 1,000 people	
1 Italy	18.2	1 Lebanon	732
2 Greece	....	2= Brunei	....
3 Sweden	17.4	2= Luxembourg	....
4 Japan	....	4 Italy	539
5 Spain	....	5 Iceland	....
6 Belgium	16.7	6 Germany	506

Audio scripts

1 Careers

🎧 1.1 (I = Interviewer, CH = Colette Hill)

I What are some of the qualities or skills needed for a successful career in business?

CH That's a difficult one because, of course, it does depend on what field you're in … but if you press me, I would offer three particular qualities, I think. Erm, first, you need to be able to get on with people. Whatever job, you're going to have colleagues and customers. You need to be able to get on with people at all levels. Second, er, you need to be adaptable; businesses go through constant change. Your role will change, as will the people you work with, even the place where you work sometimes. And finally, of course, you need a sense of humour to keep it all in proportion.

🎧 1.2 (I = Interviewer, CH = Colette Hill)

I What are the best ways to prepare for a job interview?

CH It really helps if you look at it from the point of view of the interviewer. So, for example, before the interview do your homework. Find out all you can about the company to show you're really interested in the opportunity. You can look up how old it is, what it does, how many people it employs, how fast it's growing. Then at the interview, help the interviewer by answering their questions fully, but sticking to the point; don't talk for too long. Let them stay in control of the agenda, I think. And then there are other things like, it's important to ask the interviewer questions which demonstrate that you are as interested in them as they are in you: for example, 'What is your medium-term plan for the company?' or 'What is your policy on training and development?' These sorts of questions show you're potentially interested in staying, not just looking for a short-term contract.

🎧 1.3

A Good morning, VTS. Which department, please?

B I'd like to speak to Carmen Diaz in human resources, please.

A Thank you. Hold on, I'll put you through.

C Hello. Human resources.

B Hello. Is that Carmen Diaz?

C Speaking.

B Yes, I'm phoning about your advert in Careers Now. Could you send me an application form, please?

C Certainly. Can I take some details? Could you give me your name and address, please?

B Yes, sure, it's Christophe Boiteaud, which is B-O-I-T-E-A-U-D. And my address is …

🎧 1.4

A Hello. Could I speak to Andrea, please?

B I'm afraid she's not here at the moment. Can I take a message?

A Yes, please. This is Jacques from Intec. Could you tell her I won't be able to make the training course on Saturday. She can call me back if there's a problem. I'm on 0191 498 0001.

B OK. Thank you. Bye.

🎧 1.5

A Hi, John. Dave here.

B Oh, hello, Dave. How are you?

A Fine, thanks. Listen, just a quick word.

B Yeah, go ahead.

A Do you think you could let me have the fax number for Workplace Solutions? I can't get through to them. Their phone's always engaged.

B I've got it here. It's 020 7756 4237.

A Sorry, I didn't catch the last part. Did you say 4227?

B No, it's 4237.

A OK. Thanks. Bye.

B No problem. Bye.

🎧 1.6 (JP = Joanna Pelc)

Extract 1

JP What's my aim? Well, to be honest, I would like to get to the top as soon as I can. I'm very ambitious. And if I get the job, I don't see why I couldn't become a director in a few years' time. That's what I really want.

Extract 2

JP I applied for the job because I think I've got a lot to offer. I'm competitive and I like to win. I know a few people think I'm difficult to work with. Maybe that's true, but I get results, that's the main thing.

🎧 1.7 (AB = Anna Belinski)

Extract 1

AB If you choose me, I'll start by improving our sales team. I want people to enjoy working in our sales department. Everyone in the team must help each other, and help me as much as possible. That way, we'll get good results.

Extract 2

AB I've got a lot of sales experience, and I've always been successful wherever I've worked, especially during the past year. I think I could lead a team well. I'm the head of our local business club, and I like organising people and telling them what to do. I'm a very fast learner. I'd enjoy going on a training course to help me do the job better.

🎧 1.8 (RK = Robert Kaminsky)

Extract 1

RK I want to do a good job for the company. I think we should expand slowly over the next five years. We're in a very competitive market, so I won't take too many risks. I think we could increase our market share in the long term, but we must be patient and realistic.

Extract 2

RK I feel I have the ability and experience to do this job. I'm a 'safe pair of hands', as they say. People respect me because I have good judgement.

2 Selling online

🎧 2.1 (I = Interviewer, SM = Simon Murdoch)

I You set up the online book-selling company which became Amazon.co.uk. What do you need to do to create a successful online business?

SM Well, there's really, erm, two big questions here, and it relates to sales and to profits. So, if I deal with the sales first, to be a successful online business you really need to, er, achieve lots of sales and for that there's many things you need to get right. It's all driven by doing a fantastic job for customers so that they tell each other and keep coming back. Er, and that's driven first, you must have a good website, and the website needs to be easy and quick to use. Er, it needs to provide lots of information about the items that you're buying. And, er, the prices on there need to be, low prices, good prices. And then, once somebody's ordered something from your website, er, you need to provide a fast delivery service which is reliable. And then, if anything should go wrong, er, it's important that you have an excellent customer service team dealing with enquiries on the phone or by e-mail. So that tends to drive the sales side of the equation.

🎧 2.2 (SM = Simon Murdoch)

SM The other key thing for being a successful online retailer is that, in the long term, you must make profits. There have been a number of high profile companies that have built a great service but then never made profits and eventually run out of cash. A good example of that is e-toys, which had a great service for selling toys online in America and in Europe, and eventually they ran out of money and had to go into liquidation, erm, and really as long as you get those two sides right you can build a successful online business.

🎧 2.3 (I = Interviewer, SM = Simon Murdoch)

I And, what would you say are the key differences between online selling and high street retailing?

SM Erm, lots of people have pointed out the parallels between the two, but I suppose the key difference is when you're selling online, it's much more like a mail order company rather than a retailer. Er, you have to have warehouses with all the goods, and then you have to send those out in the post or by delivery, erm, couriers and the difference when you're a retailer on the high street is that it's much more about having the right location and when people come into your shop, presenting the items in an attractive way that gets them to buy.

🎧 2.4 (M = Michelle, D = Designer)

M Let's talk about the time for setting up the website. We want it in a month's time. That's the end of July.

D It's a bit early. I was hoping to have two months to do the job. If I finish in one month, will you agree to reduce the number of pages?

M Yes, that's no problem. Just do the best you can. Our priority is to have the website up and running as soon as possible.

D OK then, agreed.

🎧 2.5 (M = Michelle, D = Designer)

M Now about payment. You want to charge us 50 dollars an hour. That works out at 400 dollars a day, I believe.

D Yes, that's the normal fee for the job.

M Well, we'd prefer to pay you a fixed amount for the work. We can offer you $6,000.

D I see. Do you mind if I ask you why you want to pay that way?

M Well, you see, that way we can control the cost of the project. If we pay you per hour, the cost could become high. It could get out of control. This way, we know where we stand.

D I see. $6,000. Mmm, that could be all right, I suppose, as long as I get some money in advance. How about paying me half when I start the work and half at the end?

M Yes, I think we could arrange that. OK. I agree to that.

🎧 2.6 (M = Michelle, D = Designer)

D Now, the design of the website. Will we have book covers on it?

M Absolutely. I'd like to display a large number of book covers on every page. They'd really attract people's attention. What do you think?

D It's a bit too much, I'd say. A lot of pictures take too long to download. I'd prefer one big image. How about that?

M Mmm, I don't know. People like to see the book covers. It draws them into the website, believe me.

D Maybe you're right. How about two covers per page, then?

M OK, that sounds reasonable. Now, what else do we need to discuss before you get started?

3 Companies

🎧 3.1 (I = Interviewer, BT = Bruno Tagliaferri)

I Bruno Tagliaferri, Triumph has been very successful in relaunching the company and increasing its sales. What are the reasons for its success?

BT Well, I think there are a number of reasons. Firstly, I think Triumph has a very strong brand name. Erm, it's a model that goes back to the early 1900s. It's possibly still one of the strongest names in motorcycling, so we've been able to build on our reputation and on the name. Secondly, we've developed new models which have attracted people's attention. We've invested a lot of money in these models, and they've helped us to compete with other companies in the motorcycle industry. The third reason for our success is, I believe, we've given the bike a very up-to-date look. We've focussed on styling and also on the quality of our product. It's taken a bit of time to build up sales, but we've done well in the first nine years, and we are now a serious alternative manufacturer.

🎧 3.2 (I = Interviewer, BT = Bruno Tagliaferri)

I Most of your sales are exports. How do you create interest abroad?

BT Well, to create interest abroad, firstly in our key markets, those are the markets with volume sales, we've got subsidiaries, so they're companies we wholly own; America, Germany and France are key motorcycle markets. From day one, we've had our own staff and local staff in subsidiaries. In other markets we've got very good distributors. So, through those two routes, subsidiaries and distributors, we have a strong dealer network. The dealers are very professional at marketing, so we can launch all of their new models with a very strong PR campaign and support the dealers' local marketing.

I What else can you tell me about your distribution in key markets?

BT We want the dealers to strongly promote motorcycling. They must have a subnetwork of dealers who are positive and enthusiastic about our company. When you're selling motorcycles, you're selling a product to people who are very knowledgeable. So you need people at a retailing level who are knowledgeable and enthusiastic about the product and able to sell it in the face of strong competition.

We've been successful in creating interest abroad. In fact, today over 80 percent of what we manufacture here goes to export markets. The key markets, the markets with the greatest potential, as I said before, are America, where Triumph Meriden traditionally sold the majority of its products; Germany, which is our largest market in Europe; and France.

🎧 3.3 (MR = Marta Rodriguez)

MR Good morning, everyone. Thanks for coming to my presentation. My name's Marta Rodriguez. I'm Personnel Director of Tara Fashions. I'm going to talk to you today about our company. First, I'll give you some basic information about Tara Fashions. Then I'll talk about our overseas stores. After that I'll outline the strengths of the company. Next I'll talk about career opportunities with Tara. And finally I'll mention our future plans. I'll be pleased to answer any questions at the end of my talk.

Let me start with some basic facts about Tara. The company started in 1978. We are a family-owned business and our head office is in Córdoba, Spain. We sell clothes for men and women, and our customers are mainly fashion-conscious people aged 20 to 35. We have 15 stores in Spain. All of the stores are very profitable.

Right, those are the basic facts.

Let me add a few figures. We have an annual turnover of about €260 million. Our net profits last year were approximately €16 million. We have a workforce of just over 2,000 employees. So those are the numbers.

Now about our overseas stores. We have 4 large stores in France and another 10 in other European countries. We are planning to open 5 new stores next year.

What are our strengths? We keep up with fashion trends. If we spot a trend, we can bring out a new design in 15 days. And we get it to the stores very quickly. We deliver to stores twice a week. And we sell our designs at the right price.

OK, now what about career opportunities? It's quite simple. If you are ambitious and fashion-conscious, we have opportunities in all areas of our business. We will welcome you with open arms.

Finally, a few words about our new project. We are planning to open a new store in New York next year – on Fifth Avenue. This will give us a foothold in the US market. We're very excited about this new development.

Well, thanks very much for listening to my talk. Are there any questions?

4 Great ideas

🎧 4.1

Great ideas are generated in different ways. Sometimes an idea may simply be when a company exploits an opportunity to extend the product range, to offer more choice to existing customers. Or a great idea could allow a company to enter a market which was closed to it before.

Companies which are prepared to spend a lot on R&D may make a breakthrough by having an original idea for a product which others later copy, for example Sony and the Walkman.

On the other hand, some products are developed in response to customer research. They come from customer ideas. These products meet a real need. Or the product does something similar to another product, but faster, so it saves time. Some people will buy new products because the product enhances their status – makes them feel more important. Other people will buy any 'green' product which reduces waste or protects the environment, even if it is more expensive.

If an idea is really good – perhaps the product fills a gap in the market – it may even win an award for innovation.

🎧 4.2 (I = Interviewer, TC = Tim Cook)

I Dr Cook, please describe some of the new ideas which your company has developed.

TC Well, Isis Innovation is a company owned by the University of Oxford, and our job is to take the ideas that have developed in the university's research laboratories and help the researchers turn them into commercial opportunities, and we do this by either negotiating licences or by helping researchers to start new companies. Some of the companies that we've recently started, for example, there's one company which uses technology developed in the engineering department to make car bodies more quickly and therefore more economically. Another company we've started makes houses for bees to help people who, er, grow fruit in orchards to grow fruit more efficiently because the bees help the trees be more productive. A third idea we've had is, we've started a company for archaeologists which trains archaeologists in the use of computer techniques, but also sells them the software that they need to do this.

🎧 4.3 (I = Interviewer, TC = Tim Cook)

I And, what stages are involved in developing an idea and bringing it to market?

TC To build a company on university science, you have to bring together a number of components. The first thing you need is a business plan, which we help the researchers to write. We can then use this business plan to raise the investment – the cash that you need to start the business. This comes from private investors who are rich individuals, usually who've made money from running their own businesses. You also need people to manage the new company and we have a database of these people and introduce them to the scientists.

🎧 4.4 (I = Inge, Ka = Katharina, Ke = Kenneth, N = Nadia, J = Julia)

I Right, can we start, please? The main aim of the meeting is to decide the date of the launch. After that, we'll talk about our marketing strategy and decide which sales outlets we should target. OK, when are we going to launch the goggles? Katharina, what do you think? Should it be early next year or should we wait until the summer?

Ka I'm in favour of February or March. There's a gap in the market for our products. Why wait any longer? The goggles are technically advanced – let's just cash in on that.

I Thanks, Katharina. OK, let's hear a few more views. Kenneth, what's your opinion?

Ke Mmm, I don't know about February. It's a bit early in the year. I suggest we launch in May or June. People go on holiday then. It's a peak period for buying goggles.

I   Thanks, Kenneth. Nadia, what's your view? You're a keen swimmer, I know.

N   In my opinion, February's the best time. We could promote them in swimming pools and opticians. The price should be high. I'd say, at least £50.

Ka   Hold on a minute. I thought we were talking about the launch date, not about promotion or price.

I   You're right, Katharina. Let's get back to the point. OK everyone, I think on balance we agree we prefer the earlier date. Let's move on now to marketing. Julia, which outlets do you think we should target?

J   I think we should start with the specialist stores. That's where most swimmers buy their goggles.

I   What do you mean by specialist stores, Julia? Are you thinking of sports goods outlets, you know, stores which only sell sports equipment?

J   Exactly. They should be our main target.

5 Stress

5.1 (I = Interviewer, CC = Cary Cooper)

I   Professor Cooper, what are the major causes of stress at work today?

CC   I think the major causes of stress at work today are firstly, increasing job insecurity, and what I mean by that is that many people these days feel they could lose their jobs, they don't feel their jobs are safe. They feel they may not have a job next month or next year. Secondly, working long hours is becoming common across the whole of Europe. There are problems with how much time people are spending at work compared to the time they spend at home – what is called the work–life balance, and how to get this balance right. In many countries, both in Europe and around the world, the typical family is a working family, with both members working, which causes problems for those families. So, working people really are experiencing problems which maybe 40 or 50 years ago they didn't have.

5.2 (I = Interviewer, CC = Cary Cooper)

I   And how can people cope successfully with stress?

CC   For people to manage stress successfully, they first have to find out the main reason for it. For example, are they stressed because the company they work for has a habit of working long hours which is causing problems in their personal life? Or is it that they have a boss who gives them orders all the time, a boss who checks their work all the time and doesn't give them freedom or independence to organise their own work? Or is it that they are a woman and they work for a company which makes it difficult for women to make progress in their career, or to get promoted because the company is not flexible in its working arrangements? Each of these problems needs a different solution, so it's important for people to find out what their particular problem is and then once they've done this to think about the possible solutions.

5.3 (I = Interviewer, CC = Cary Cooper)

I   Do you think that men and women deal with stress differently?

CC   In my opinion men and women do deal with stress in different ways. Women are more flexible, and are able to change the way they behave and do things when they're in new situations which they have to deal with.

They also seem to cope with the pressures better than men. For example, now there are many working women around the world, you find that women have a double pressure on them. Often they have to look after children, work in the home – do the cooking and cleaning – as well as work in a paying job. So, women have more pressure than men. But, if you look at the number of people who become ill from stress, you find that the number of women is less than men. This is because women are able to manage stress better than men. Women have a number of strategies to do this. What are these strategies? Well, they have the ability to express emotion, which men find difficult to do. Also, they are able to seek social help when they're in trouble – to go to people and talk about their problems. And in general women don't pretend that problems don't exist.

5.4 (V = Vincent, M = Monica, T = Tanya)

V   I think we should do a lot more to improve our staff's health and fitness. What do you think, Monica?

M   I agree. There are all sorts of things we could do to help staff to become more healthy and stay healthy. For one thing, we could offer them a free medical checkup every year.

V   Right. That's a good idea. A lot of firms do that. And how about having a no-smoking policy in the staff restaurant? What do you think about that, Tanya?

T   Mm, I don't think I like the idea very much. It wouldn't be good for morale. A lot of our staff smoke – they'd be against it, I'm sure of that. I think we should improve the food. A lot of the dishes aren't healthy – there's far too much fatty food, not enough fish, fruit and vegetables.

V   True. We could change the menus and offer healthier meals. I like that idea.

M   What about setting up a counselling service, Vincent? Some staff are under a lot of stress. It affects their work and they need professional help.

V   I don't know, Monica. It'd be very expensive to set up a service like that. Anyway, we have a company doctor. That's her job, isn't it?

5.5 (V = Vincent, T = Tanya, M = Monica)

V   I've got another suggestion. We could talk to the manager of our local sports centre and arrange a company membership. What do you think, Tanya?

T   Mm, I don't know. It sounds interesting, but it could be very expensive. A group fee for all our staff would probably cost a fortune.

V   What's your opinion, Monica?

M   I think you're right, Tanya. It'd cost a lot and I'm not sure how many staff would actually use the centre. Some people say it hasn't got many facilities.

V   I can't agree with you there. It's got a very good pool and sauna. If we could negotiate a low membership fee, it might be worth considering, surely.

T   Yes, it's worth checking out, I suppose. A lot of staff might enjoy having a swim at lunchtime or after work. And a sauna is very relaxing, I must admit.

M   Maybe, but there are so many other things we could do. Things which are less expensive, but they'd improve people's health just as much. Let me tell you about a few ideas I have …

6 ...ertaining

(... = Inte... = Tony Barnard)

...do co... money on corporate
...ainin...
...riet... er, but I think the single, most
... modern companies,
... re operating what I call a
... ...agement programme',
...run... ...gramme the human content
...tha... ...portant. And ... ...ny
...es... that ... ...ur or five
... ...s to keep an
... ...s become a very
... ...lationship
... forms of entertaining
... ...sting that you've been
... 'the big six' events as I call them, will
...ver popular and I'm talking about the
...is Championships, Royal Ascot, the
...erm, Henley Royal Regatta, Chelsea
...ow, erm, and the Grand Prix. These are
...ts which will sell out year-in, year-out. But more
...d more new events are happening all the time –
hospitality at music events is becoming more popular.
We've always traditionally had the opera, but we now
have jazz events or even rock and pop events where
people take and entertain their clients, both inside and
outside.

🎧 6.2 (I = Interviewer , TB = Tony Barnard)

I   And, what types of company spend money on
entertaining – is it only the large ones?

TB No, not at all. Right across the corporate spectrum,
companies spend money on entertaining, for the
reason I said earlier on, about customer relationship
management. It doesn't matter if you're a small
business or you're a multinational. You need to retain
your clients and customers if you are to grow your
business, and particularly, the emphasis might be more
on a small business – you may have fewer number of
customers, so if you lose a big … a big client it could
hurt you quite badly. And people say to me, that isn't
corporate entertaining a barometer of the economy?
In other words, if the economy starts to decline, they
will decline their spend on entertaining. That's no
longer true either, because actually it's equally
important, if not more so, to retain your customers in
times of economic decline than in times of economic
boom.

🎧 6.3

Conversation 1

A   Hello, I'm Liz.
B   Oh, hello again, Liz. How are you? It's Jane; we met in
Paris last year.
A   Oh yes, I didn't recognise you. Your hair's different.
I'm fine, and what about you?
B   I'm very well thanks.
A   And how's business?
B   It's going well, especially in Italy.
A   Great.

Conversation 2

A   James, have you met Sam Clarke?
B   No. Hello, Sam. Good to meet you. I think we both
know Bill Carlton. I used to work with him in Spain.

C   Oh, yes … Bill. He's in Moscow now.
B   Really? I didn't know that. Give him my regards next
time you see him.
C   Yes, I will.

Conversation 3

A   Julia, do you know Jurgen?
B   Yes, of course. Hello, Jurgen. Good to see you again.
How are things?
C   Fine thanks, Julia. It's great to see you.

Conversation 4

A   Hi, I'm John.
B   Hello, John. Pleased to meet you. I'm Lisa from the
Munich office.
A   Oh, Munich. I've never been, but I hear it's a great city,
very lively.
B   Yes, it is. It's great. You should come. The conference is
going to be there next year.
A   I'd love to. I'll look forward to it.

Conversation 5

A   Carla, I'd like you to meet one of our best customers,
Linda Eriksson from SRT in Sweden.
B   Hello, Linda. Nice to meet you. I've heard a lot about
you.
C   Not all bad I hope!
B   Not at all. It's good to be able to put a face to a name.
C   Absolutely!

7 Marketing

🎧 7.1

A   I really wanted it, but when I tried to buy it, I just
couldn't get it anywhere. My friend heard that it was in
one shop and he queued up for ages, but they'd run
out by lunchtime.
B   The company held a party on a river boat to launch
their new campaign. It was absolutely fantastic. We
also got a free gift at the end.
C   The shoes were really expensive but definitely worth it.
I think the fact that they are so expensive really
distinguishes them from the competition.
D   I've had this briefcase for 20 years and it still looks
good. The material is high quality and long-lasting.

🎧 7.2 (I = Interviewer, MI = Mirjana Ilic)

I   Mirjana, what is the key to successful marketing?
MI Well, the key to successful marketing involves many
different things. Most people would say successful
marketing is just a good creative campaign. Some
people would go further than that and say it involves
many good marketing communications, reaching the
right people, clear marketing messages, and working
well with sales teams to get the right sales channels.
But the most common definition of marketing is just
two words: customer orientation. What does that
actually mean though? It really means four things:
producing what customers want, when they want it, at
the right price and in a way that's profitable for the
company, and I believe in that definition very strongly.

🎧 7.3 (I = Interviewer, MI = Mirjana Ilic)

I   Could you describe a marketing campaign that
impressed you?
MI Well, marketing is very much in my blood and it's my
first love, so there are lots of campaigns I come across
every day that really impress me. But I think the most
memorable in recent years has been the Orange mobile

phone campaign, partly because the whole area of mobile technologies and mobile communications I find very interesting and incredibly exciting, but partly because it was a great campaign in itself. It has the fantastic strap line 'the future's bright, the future's orange', which is so memorable and so meaningful for all segments of the population.

🎧 7.4 (I = Interviewer, MI = Mirjana Ilic)

I Could you give an example of an unsuccessful campaign?

MI Well, I think the most unsuccessful recent campaign for me was the one where an electrical goods manufacturer tried to roll out a very simple sales promotion. Initially, if you bought any electrical appliance over a certain value, you were promised free flights with every purchase. Now, although initially this campaign did seem to be quite successful because sales went up, in the end they had to stop the campaign because they simply couldn't keep up with the demand and they were overspending a lot on these prizes. So I think basically, from the early stages the campaign was badly planned, badly budgeted and it resulted in a lot of negative publicity for the company.

🎧 7.5

1
A 2 5 5 2 5 2
2
B 8 8 1 9 9 0
3
C 020 8045 1930
4
D 00 33 2399 5324

🎧 7.6

A B C D E F G H I J K L M N O P Q R S T U V W X Y Z

🎧 7.7 (M = Martin, F = Fiona)

F Hello.
M Hello, Fiona. This is Martin. How are things going?
F Fine, thanks.
M I haven't received your sales report yet for the quarter. Any problems?
F Oh, no. Sorry, Martin. I've been really busy lately. But I can tell you, we've had excellent results.
M Good.
F Yeah. We've met our sales targets and increased our market share by two percent. Our total sales were over £1.2 million.
M Over 1.2 million. Great! Well done! What about the new range of shampoos?
F Well, we had a very successful product launch. We spent £30,000 on advertising it and …
M Sorry, did you say 13,000?
F No, 30,000. We advertised in the national press, took out space in trade magazines and did a number of presentations to our distributors. It was money well spent. We've had a lot of orders already and good comments from customers.
M I'm really pleased to hear that.

🎧 7.8 (M = Martin, F = Fiona)

M Anything else to report?
F Yes, there is one thing. One of my biggest customers will be visiting London next week. She'd like to have a meeting with you.
M Fine. Could you give me a few details? What's her name?
F It's Mrs Young Joo Chan.
M Sorry, I didn't catch that.
F Young Joo Chan. I'll spell that for you. Y-O-U-N-G J-O-O C-H-A-N. She's Korean actually. She's chief buyer for HDS. Let me give you her telephone number: 82 2 0735 8879. OK? Why not give her a ring? She's expecting to hear from you.
M I'll do that. But first, let me read that back to you. It's Young Joo Chan from HDS. Telephone number 82 2 0735 8875.
F No, 82 2 0735 8879.
M OK, I've got that. Just one more thing. Did she say when she'd like to meet?
F Yes, she said next Thursday or Friday – that's the 17th or 18th.
M What about Friday the 18th? I'll give her a call. Right, I think that's everything.
F Fine. I'll get that report to you by the end of the week.
M Right. Bye for now.
F Bye.

🎧 7.9 (I = Interviewer)

I Have you ever bought Kristal bottled water?
A Yes, I tried it when I saw it on television.
I What did you think of it?
A Nothing special. Just like any other water, but a bit more expensive.

I Kristal is more expensive than some other bottled waters. Do you think it's worth paying extra for this brand of water?
B Not really. It's got a fresh taste, I suppose.
I Do you think it's healthier than other bottled waters?
B Well, they say it is in the advertising. It could be, but I don't really know. I'll tell you in 40 years' time.

I Do you buy Kristal bottled water regularly?
C No. I can't find it in the supermarkets. If it's not in the supermarkets, where am I supposed to buy it?

I When I say Kristal bottled water, what word do you think of?
D Expensive. I haven't tried it because I can get a similar bottled water for half the price.

I Have you tried Kristal water?
E I've never heard of it. Where can you buy it?

8 Planning

🎧 8.1

Recently we decided to open a new sales office in New York. First I arranged a meeting with the finance department to discuss the project. We prepared a budget with details of the various costs involved. Then we collected information about possible locations for the new office. We considered two options – one in Greenwich Village and the other near Central Park. After doing some more research, I wrote a report for the board of directors.

Unfortunately, we made a mistake when we estimated the costs as the exchange rate changed, and so we didn't keep within our budget. We overspent by almost 20 percent. We had to rearrange the schedule for moving into the building because the office was not redecorated in time. The board of directors was unhappy because we didn't meet the deadline for opening the office by 15 December. It finally opened in January. However, we forecast sales of at least $500,000 in the first year.

🎧 **8.2 (I = Interviewer, RS = Rebecca Stephens)**

I Rebecca, your business is climbing mountains, and good planning is really important. What's the secret of good planning?

RS The most important thing is to know exactly what it is that you want to achieve, and define it, and define by when you want to achieve it and with that information, you can then set a deadline and identify the tasks that are necessary to achieve that goal, basically get on with them to a timetable.

🎧 **8.3 (I = Interviewer, RS = Rebecca Stephens)**

I And can you tell us about something that you planned well?

RS I was reasonably happy with my planning of 'the seven summits', which was a project to climb the highest mountain on each of the seven continents. Everest was one of those – having climbed that, I had four remaining mountains in order to achieve that goal, and time was important for reasons of sponsorship, so I had to work back from the last mountain, which was in Antarctica, which I couldn't climb until the month of November, so the other three mountains, I had to fit in between January, when I set out to do this, and November, the date of the last mountain. And key to it, really, was communication with the people that I was climbing with; they were scattered around the world and it was important to keep them in touch so they knew exactly what was to be achieved and by when.

🎧 **8.4 (I = Interviewer, RS = Rebecca Stephens)**

I Plans sometimes go wrong. In business, what should people do if this happens?

RS There are some things which are clearly outside our control. On a mountain, it's very clearly the weather – in business it might often be unforeseen changes in the economic climate, and I think we can all do ourselves a favour by not worrying too much about that, accepting that. But, having said that, it's important when things change, and sometimes not for the better, to step back, reassess the situation and redefine one's goal. It might even mean changing one's end goal, but always knowing exactly what it is that you want to achieve is the important thing.

🎧 **8.5**

A We need to decide exactly when we're going to move. Any suggestions?

B I think July would be the best time. It's very quiet then, isn't it?

A You mean, we don't do too much business then.

B Exactly. Our sales are always down that month and quite a few staff are away on holiday. We could move all the office equipment at the weekend. Do everything at once. That's the best way …

C Could I just say something?

B Go ahead.

C I think we should take longer to move. A weekend's too short. In my opinion we should do it department by department.

B How do you mean, exactly?

C Well, each week a different department would move. That way, there would always be people here who could handle customer enquiries, phone calls, and so on.

B Hmm, I see what you mean. Maybe it would be better to phase the move over several weeks. Of course, we'll have to keep our staff informed at every stage of the move. We can do that mainly by internal e-mail. Now, moving on to the question of transport. We've contacted two companies, National Transport and Fox Removals.

A Sorry, could I just comment on that, Mark?

B Certainly.

A I don't think it would be a good idea to use National. I've heard one or two things about them – I don't think they're too reliable. But Fox would be fine. They've got an excellent reputation in the trade.

B OK, perhaps it would be better to use Fox then. You know, there's another possibility. We could get our own people to do the moving.

A What? You think our transport department could do the job?

B Why not? They're not too busy in July.

A I don't think that's a good idea. This is a really big job. We need a specialised firm for that like Fox. They've got the experience and will do a good job, even if it does cost us a bit more. Also, Fox offers a free consultation service.

B Mmm, you're probably right. I'll call Fox and discuss the relocation with them. I'll see if I can persuade them to lower their price a little.

🎧 **8.6**

A I'd like a really interesting report on an important business topic. Something that makes you think. Plenty of facts and details. If a company's having problems, give us all the information. If there's a new tax affecting business, tell us all about it.

B I think the presenters should be two young people with lots of personality, who know a bit about business. A male and female – that'd be perfect.

C Please, please, don't be BORING. What about a funny story, something light which will make us laugh on our way to work?

D The programme must be lively. Maybe you could have a topic for the day and get people to phone in with their opinions. Then we could talk about it at work.

E We'd all like short interviews with important people. Maybe some advice – they could talk about mistakes they had made and how to avoid them.

9 Managing people

🎧 **9.1 (I = Interviewer, KN = Kriengsak Niratpattanasai)**

I Kriengsak, what do managers need in order to be good managers of people?

KN Well, I think good managers need to be good at four things, really. First of all, they need to be good at observing – that's so they can understand the behaviour, the strengths and weaknesses of their staff. The second thing is, I suppose, that they need to be good at listening – so they can learn about their staff's problems. The next thing is, it's important for them to be good at asking questions – so they can find out all the information they need to make the right decisions. And last of all, I think they have to be good at speaking so they can communicate their objectives clearly to all their staff.

🎧 **9.2 (I = Interviewer, KN = Kriengsak Niratpattanasai)**

I Managing international teams can present many challenges. What qualities and skills should international managers have?

KN Well, if you manage international teams, then it's really important to spend enough time preparing yourself for managing those international teams. Learn as much as you can about their language, their culture and the local conditions. And you also need to spend plenty of time with the local people. Don't try to be an expert in the first three months or so. You should take time to observe and to learn and ask questions.

9.3 (I = Interviewer, KN = Kriengsak Niratpattanasai)

I What mistakes do foreign managers make when managing Asian staff, for example Thais and Chinese?

KN Well, some international managers want their Asian staff to be more forceful. Another thing is, they want them to be able to deal with problems logically. And they want their staff to be ambitious like them. I think they sometimes ignore the background, the education and the cultural differences between themselves and their staff. They may underestimate the skills and abilities of their local staff because they are focussing too much on their weaknesses. The managers have a tendency to jump to conclusions too quickly, and they tend to label all local staff as being the same.

9.4

1

A This is Jenny. I'm ringing about the conference. Great news! I've found a hotel with good rates. So how many rooms do you want to book?

2

B Hi. This is Jason. I'm phoning about the management training course. I want to confirm my place on the course. By the way, who's leading it? Thanks.

3

C Oh hello. This is Carol. I'm ringing about next Friday's meeting. I've got two questions. Firstly, how many people will there be at the meeting and secondly, what time will it finish? OK? Bye.

4

D Hi. This is Maria from Finance. I'm phoning about the budget. How much did you spend on the Tokyo trip? I need to fill in the expenses claim by Friday.

9.5 (A = Alexandra, R = Rachel)

A What are you planning this evening, Rachel?

R Nothing really. Maybe I'll look over my notes for tomorrow's presentation.

A Look, why don't you relax a little? I'm going to a restaurant tonight with a few colleagues – you've met one or two of them – would you like to come with us? It's in the town centre. We could have a few drinks afterwards.

R Well, it's very kind of you, Alexandra, but I think I'd like to relax at the hotel tonight, if you don't mind. I'm a bit tired, quite honestly.

A Are you sure? You'd really enjoy it.

R It's very kind of you, but perhaps another time.

9.6 (M = Marta, S = Sven)

M I don't know too much about Sweden really, Sven. What do people here like doing in their spare time?

S Well, Marta, Swedish people like to be in the open air. They're very health conscious. So, they enjoy playing sports, football, tennis, skiing and ice-skating in the winter. And of course a lot of people have summer cottages, by the sea or lakes. So they go there at the weekends and relax, swim, go sailing, and so on.

M Interesting. And what about you, Sven, what do you usually do after work? In the evenings?

S I usually watch television. And often I have a sauna with my family. We enjoy that a lot. How about you, Marta?

M Well, generally I spend time with my children, and read to them before they go to bed. After that, I sit down, chat to my husband, and then we argue about what to watch on television!

9.7 (M = Marta, S = Sven)

M I've really enjoyed the trip, Sven. I'm sure we'll be doing a lot of business together in future.

S Yes, there's a lot of potential in Sweden for your products, and we can help you build up sales here.

M Good, I think so too. Thanks very much for your hospitality. I really enjoyed the meal tonight. And also thanks for showing me round the city yesterday. It was fascinating. I feel I know Stockholm a bit now.

S I'm glad you enjoyed the tour, Marta. We're very proud of our city, as you may know. Well, I hope you have a good journey back. We'll be in touch soon, I'm sure.

M Yes, I'll call you as soon as I've talked to my colleagues about your proposal. We'll take it from there.

S Goodbye, Marta. All the best.

M Bye, Sven.

10 Conflict

10.1 (I = Interviewer, JK = Jeremy Keeley)

I Jeremy, could you give me an example of where conflict was handled badly?

JK Yes, I can. The example I'm thinking about is of two professional managers in a team, erm, who were constantly arguing with each other. Erm, the rest of the team avoided the problem and eventually the frustrations built up such that there was a huge great fight with lots of things said that shouldn't have been said, and the reason the conflict was badly managed was that everybody avoided the problem. Everybody tried to make everybody feel better rather than actually saying look, we have an issue here. Let's address the issue.

10.2 (I = Interviewer, JK = Jeremy Keeley)

I Could you give me an example of where conflict was handled well?

JK Yes. An example I can quote is one that I personally was involved in where a colleague at work and I had certain problems with each other. She had a way of working that I wasn't comfortable with and I was showing my frustration by being aggressive and assertive, and we sorted the conflict out in a very constructive way because she addressed it with me directly. She asked me what was wrong, she listened to me carefully. She played back that she really understood my problems and concerns and then constructively we worked out a way together quickly.

10.3 (GM = General Manager, UR = Union Representative)

GM We just don't have enough spaces for everyone. We need the spaces for managers and customers who visit us. Sorry, Tracy, but that's it.

UR Well, you'll have to think again. Our staff arrive early. They need somewhere to park.

GM Look, Tracy, I understand what you're saying, but it just isn't possible anymore.

UR Well, that's a typical management attitude. The staff

are not going to accept it. I warn you, Tom, this could lead to a strike.

GM Oh come on, Tracy… you know we've got a parking problem. We've got to do something about it. OK, how about this? What if we keep five spaces for staff, and it's first come, first served.

UR Sorry, that isn't good enough. It's not a solution to the parking problem, and you know it.

GM There is another possibility. How about if the staff park their cars in the car park near the station?

UR Some of them do that already. But they have to pay quite a bit, you know. The cost goes up every six months. You can't expect everyone to do that, surely.

GM OK, Tracy. What if we could help towards the cost? We might be able to pay, say, thirty percent.

UR Yes … it's worth considering. It might help.

GM Right. I'll discuss this proposal at the next board meeting. Staff will park in the public car park, and we'll contribute thirty percent towards the cost.

UR Fine. That's it then.

10.4 (OM = Olivier Moyon, TF = Todd Foster)

OM I've been thinking a lot recently, Todd. I think you probably know, I'm not happy here at all. And I feel I've got to do something about it.

TF Really? What exactly is the problem?

OM I think you know it, Todd. Jacques let me down badly with that order. He just wouldn't make any effort for me, so we've lost the order. It means I don't get the commission and it'll also affect my bonus.

TF Olivier, you must understand, you can't promise a customer that we'll deliver in three weeks. It's a busy time at the moment. Jacques's working under a lot of pressure.

OM Maybe, but let's face it, Jacques's no good as a production manager. He can't deal with pressure. He just says, 'Sorry, I can't help.' But it's not just Jacques …

TF Oh yes?

OM Well, to be honest, I'm not happy with the way you run the department.

TF I'm listening.

OM The trouble with you is, you always want to know where I am, every second of the day. You give me no space. You want to control me all the time. How can I meet my sales targets if I have to spend all the time writing reports, answering your telephone messages and attending meetings? I've got to be out there selling, twenty-four hours a day.

TF Maybe, but you can't just do what you like, when you like, Olivier. Discipline is important …

OM Discipline! Control! Look, I've had enough. I've given everything to this company. But no one cares. So, I've decided to resign. You'll get my letter in the morning and I'll send a copy to Charles. He won't be pleased, I'm sure. We've been friends for years. But I just can't work with you, Todd. There's no other solution.

11 New business

11.1

The economy is stable following the problems of the past two years. By following a tight monetary policy the government has reduced the inflation rate to 2 percent. After going up dramatically, the interest rate is now down to 8 percent. The last six months has seen a slight improvement in the exchange rate against the dollar. The GDP has grown by 0.15 percent. Exports are increasing

and the balance of trade is starting to look much healthier. The unemployment rate continues to be a problem as it is still 16 percent. In order to stimulate the economy and attract foreign investment the government is offering new tax incentives as well as making a renewed effort to reduce government bureaucracy. Finally, a large skilled labour force means there could be attractive investment opportunities over the next five years.

11.2 (I = Interviewer, YT = Yvonne Thompson)

I What advice do you give to people starting their own companies?

YT When you're starting your own company, you have to be very confident. You have to be very determined. You have to know what it is you're doing. You need to research the business – or the business arena that you're intending to go into. You need to research your competitors and benchmark your service or your product against your competitors. You need good family backup. You need good backup from your friends. And probably the most important thing is that you need a good mentor, and that needs to be a business mentor as well as a personal mentor.

11.3 (YT = Yvonne Thompson)

YT You need a really good business plan. Again, you need to make sure that whatever you put on your business plan, you need to check it on a regular basis, whether it's weekly, monthly, six months or every year and you need to gauge where you are with what your business plan says. You need a very good relationship with your bank and your bank manager. But to me the most important thing is a really good marketing campaign, because if you don't have a marketing campaign that ensures that your customers know where you are, you won't have a business for very long.

11.4

I usually get to work before my boss arrives and as soon as I arrive I check my e-mail and post. I usually try to answer all important enquiries before I go to lunch. While I'm having lunch, I often discuss problems with colleagues. When I work long hours, I can take time off another day. I have a lot of flexibility over when I arrive at the office and when I leave, depending on the daily workload.

11.5 See Course Book, page 103.

11.6

1

And here is the business news. This month inflation is up by 1.2 percent. The unemployment rate is now 5 percent giving an overall figure of 1,258,000.

2

Laser plc, the supermarket giant, reports that profits rose 12 percent to just over $1.8 billion, with sales increasing a healthy 18 percent.

3

General Engineering said it would reduce its workforce by one-third over the next five years, resulting in the loss of 5,000 jobs.

4

The Central Bank has reduced interest rates by 0.5 percent. Turning to the world economy, this will grow by 2.8 percent next year.

12 Products

⌒ 12.1

1 The best thing I've ever bought is my camera because I can look back at all my travels and the people I've met, and it brings back memories that I can enjoy all my life.

2 The best thing I've ever bought is a train ticket to Brighton because I met the love of my life as I was queuing in the buffet car.

3 Last week I bought some speakers for my Mac computer. They cost about £40, which is really good value. You just plug them into your computer and get sound as good as many hi-fis. This means I don't have to buy a DVD player to watch films as I can do it on the computer and have a great sound.

4 My very expensive Prada bag. It was a luxury buy. I was attracted by its style and it cost me a lot of money, far more than I would have spent before, but it's extremely well-made and I suppose you could say it's a timeless classic. I use it every day. It looks good in every situation and for every occasion.

5 I bought a tree seven years ago for my son's birth. It cost £30. Now it's a magnificent tree. Its leaves change colour with the seasons. It provides shade; it's a home for birds. When it's bigger I'm going to build a tree house for the children to play in.

⌒ 12.2

This is our new product – a CD tower system. As you can see, it's attractive and stylish. The tower is made of wood and it holds twenty CDs. Let me tell you its dimensions. It's 33 centimetres high, 18 centimetres long and 20 centimetres wide. It comes in three colours: black, brown and white. And its selling price is just under £25 – a very competitive price.

It's ideal for storing CDs and CD-Roms. It has several special features which should appeal to our customers. Firstly it has a soft-touch mechanism. This means you just touch a button and the CD comes out smoothly and quietly. Another advantage is that it's easy to select the CD you want because the title is clearly displayed. A very useful feature too is that it's simple to use. You can open the CD case without taking it off its tray.

The tower is well-designed. It's robust, elegant and user-friendly. It's very flexible – I forgot to mention that – because the towers are modular, so you can put one on top of the other. That's a big advantage for people who have lots of CDs. And one other thing, you can save £15 if you buy two units instead of one.

I think the CD tower will be one of our best-selling products. It really does meet the needs of music lovers. It's so practical, it's a high-quality product, and great value for money.

Are there any questions you'd like to ask?

Glossary of business terms

Adjective *(adj)* Headwords for adjectives followed by information in square brackets [only before a noun] and [not before a noun] show any restrictions on where they can be used.

Noun *(n)* The codes [C] and [U] show whether a noun, or a particular sense of a noun, is countable (an agenda, two agendas) or uncountable (absenteeism, advertising).

Verbs *(v)* The forms of irregular verbs are given after the headword. The codes [I] (intransitive) and [T] (transitive) show whether a verb, or a particular sense of a verb, has or does not have an object. **Phrasal verbs** *(phr v)* are shown after the verb they are related to.

Some entries show information on words that are related to the headword. **Adverbs** *(adv)* are often shown in this way after adjectives.

Region labels The codes *AmE* and *BrE* show whether a word or sense of a word is used only in American English or British English.

---

absenteeism *n* [U] the problem of employees not being at work when they should be

accessory *n* [C] a small thing that you add to a house, clothes etc to make them look more attractive

account *n* 1 [C] an arrangement between a customer and a bank that allows the customer to pay in and take out money
2 **accounts** [plural] the official financial records of a company, person etc

accountant *n* [C] a professional whose job is to keep the financial records of an organization, or to advise clients on financial and tax matters

ad *n* [C] an informal word for advertisement

administration *n* [U] the activity of managing and organizing the work of a company or organization

advert *n* [C] *BrE* an informal word for advertisement

advertise *v* [I,T] 1 to tell people publicly about a product or service in order to persuade them to buy it
2 to inform people publicly that a job is available and invite them to apply for it

advertisement *n* [C] a picture, piece of writing, or film that tells people about a product or service in order to persuade them to buy it

advertiser *n* [C] a person or organization that advertises their products or services

advertising *n* [U] 1 telling people about a product or service in order to persuade them to buy it
2 the companies that prepare and sell advertising, considered as an industry

advertising campaign *n* [C] an organization's programme of advertising activities over a particular period with specific aims, for example to increase sales of a product

agenda *n* [C] 1 a list of the subjects to be discussed at a meeting
2 the things that someone considers important or that they are planning to do something about

aggressive *adj* 1 an aggressive plan or action is intended to achieve its result by using direct and forceful methods
2 an aggressive person or organization is very determined to achieve what they want

application *n* [C] 1 a formal, usually written, request for something, especially a job, a place at university, or permission to do something
2 a practical use for something
3 a piece of software for a particular use or job

apply *v* 1 [I] to make a formal, usually written request for something, especially a job, a place at university, or permission to do something
2 [T] to use something such as a law or an idea in a particular situation, activity, or process

appoint *v* [T] to choose someone for a particular job

appointment *n* 1 [C] an arrangement to meet someone at a particular place or time
2 [C,U] the act of choosing someone for a particular job, or the job itself

approximate *adj* an approximate amount, number etc is a little more or a little less than the exact amount, number etc – **approximately** *adv*

assertive *adj* behaving in a confident way in order to get what you want

asset *n* 1 [C] something of value belonging to a person or company that has value or the power to earn money
2 **assets** [plural] the property, equipment etc owned by a business considered together, as shown in its balance sheet

attend *v* [I,T] to go to an event such as a meeting

award *n* [C] a prize for good performance in a particular activity

background *n* 1 [C] someone's past, for example their education, qualifications, and the jobs they have had
2 [C,U] information about events in the past that explain the current situation

balance of trade *n* [singular] the difference between the value of a country's exports and its imports

balance sheet *n* [C] a document showing a company's financial position at a particular time

bankrupt *adj* not having enough money to pay your debts – **bankruptcy** *n* [C,U]

bargain[1] *n* [C] 1 something you buy cheaply or for less than its usual price
2 an agreement between two people to do something in return for something else

bargain[2] *v* [I] to discuss the conditions of a sale, agreement etc in order to get the greatest advantage for yourself – **bargaining** *n* [U]

benchmark *n* [C] 1 something that can be used as a comparison to judge or measure other things
2 a good performance in a particular activity by one company that can be used as a standard to judge the same activity in other companies – **benchmark** *v* [T], **benchmarking** *n* [U]

bill *n* [C] the total cost of something, or the document that shows this

board also **board of directors** *n* [C usually singular] the group of people who have been elected by shareholders to manage a company

bond *n* [C] a financial certificate showing an amount borrowed by an organization or government at a particular rate of interest for a particular period

bonus *n* [C] an extra amount of money added to an employee's wages, usually as a reward for doing difficult work or for doing their work well

boom[1] *n* [C,U] 1 a time when business activity increases rapidly, so that the demand for goods and services increases, prices and wages go up, and unemployment falls
2 a time when activity on the stock market reaches a high level and share prices are very high

boom[2] *v* [I] if business, trade, or the economy is booming, it is very successful and growing

branch *n* [C] an individual bank, office, shop etc that is part of a larger organization

brand[1] *n* [C] a name given to a product or group of products by a company for easy recognition

brand[2] *v* [T] to give a name to a product or group of products for easy recognition – **branding** *n* [U]

bribery *n* [U] dishonestly giving money to someone to persuade them to do something to help you – **bribe** *n* [C]

budget[1] *n* [C] an amount of money that an organization has available to spend on something in a particular period

budget[2] *v* [I,T] to plan the amounts of money to be spent on different things in a particular period

bureaucracy *n* 1 [C] a system of government that involves a large number of departments and officials
2 [U] *disapproving* all the complicated rules and processes of an official system, especially when they are confusing or responsible for causing a delay

campaign *n* [C] a series of activities designed to achieve a particular result

capacity *n* 1 [C,U] the amount of space that a container, room etc has
2 [singular, U] the amount of something that a company, factory etc can deal with or produce

capital *n* [U] money invested in something in order to make a profit

career *n* [C] 1 a profession or job that you train for
2 the series of jobs that you do during your working life

career ladder *n* [singular] all the increasingly important jobs that someone has, or would like to have, as they get older

cash *n* [U] money, especially money that is immediately available in banknotes, coins, bank accounts etc

cash flow also **cashflow** *n* 1 [U] the amounts of money coming into and going out of a company, and the timing of these
2 [C,U] profit made during a particular period, measured in different ways by different businesses

catalogue *BrE* **catalog** *AmE n* [C] a book with all of a company's products or services listed and described

chain *n* [C] a number of shops, hotels, or cinemas belonging to the same organization

chair *n* [singular] 1 the position of being the chairperson of a company or organization or the person who is chairperson
2 the position of being in charge of a meeting, or the person who is in charge of it – **chair** *v* [T]

chairman *plural* **-men**, **chairwoman** *plural* **-women** *n* [C] the most important person on the board of directors of a company, especially in the UK. In the US, this person is usually called the president of the company

chamber of commerce *n* [C] an organization made up of businesspeople in a particular place, that helps businesses with advice, support etc

charge[1] *n* 1 [C,U] the amount of money you have to pay for goods or services
2 **be in charge of sth** to be the person who controls or manages an activity or a group of people

charge[2] *v* [I,T] to ask someone to pay a particular amount of money for something

chief executive *n* [C] the manager with the most authority in the day-to-day management of a company

Chief Executive Officer (CEO) *n* [C usually singular] the title of the manager with the most authority in the day-to-day management of a company, used especially in the US. The job of CEO is sometimes combined with that of president

client *n* [C] someone who pays for professional services

colleague *n* [C] someone you work with, used especially by professional people and managers

commercial[1] *adj* 1 relating to business
2 a commercial product or service is sold in order to make a profit

commercial[2] *n* [C] an advertisement on television or radio

commission *n* [C,U] an amount of money paid to someone according to the value of goods, services, investments etc they have sold

compensation *n* [U] 1 an amount paid to someone because they have been hurt or harmed
2 the total amount of pay and benefits that an employee receives, especially a high-level manager

compete *v* [I] if a company, country etc competes with others, it tries to persuade people to buy its products or services rather than those of the others

competition *n* 1 [U] a situation where businesses or countries are competing with each other
2 [C] an event where people have to answer questions etc in order to win prizes

competitive *adj* 1 used to describe situations where companies, countries etc are competing
2 a competitive price is similar to or less than other companies' prices

competitive advantage *n* [C] something that helps you to be better or more successful than others

competitor *n* [C] a person, product, company, country etc that is competing with another

component *n* [C] a part of a product, activity etc

concept *n* [C] an idea for a product, business etc

conglomerate *n* [C] a large business organization consisting of different companies, often involved in different activities

consume *v* [T] to use raw materials, finished products etc

consumer *n* [C] a person who buys products or services for their own use, rather than to use in business or to resell

consumer behaviour *BrE* **consumer behavior** *AmE n* [U] how, why, where, and when consumers buy things, and the study of this

contract *n* [C] a formal agreement between two or more people or organizations to do something, for example to buy something

corporate *adj* [only before a noun] relating to companies, usually large ones

counselling *BrE* **counseling** *AmE n* [U] when people are given advice to help them in a difficult situation

counsellor *BrE* **counselor** *AmE n* [C] someone whose job is to give counselling

counterpart *n* [C] your counterpart is someone with the same job as you in another organization

crash[1] *n* [C] 1 a time when many investments lose their value very quickly
2 an occasion when a computer or computer software suddenly and unexpectedly stops working or fails to work properly

crash[2] *v* 1 [I] if stock markets, shares etc crash, they suddenly lose a lot of value
2 [I,T] if a computer crashes, or if you crash a computer, it suddenly and unexpectedly stops working

create *v* [T] to make something that did not exist before

creative *adj* producing or using new ideas – **creativity** *n* [U]

credit *n* [U] 1 borrowed money that is available to spend
2 an arrangement with a shop, supplier etc to buy something now and pay later

CRM abbreviation for customer relationship management

cultural *adj* 1 relating to artistic activities such as theatre, classical music etc
2 relating to the ideas, beliefs, and customs that are shared and accepted by people in a society, company etc

culture *n* [C,U] the ideas, beliefs, and customs that are shared and accepted by people in a society, company etc

currency *n* [C,U] the money used in a particular country

customer *n* [C] a person or organization that buys products

customer loyalty *n* [U] when customers continue to buy a particular company's product, and do not change to other companies' products

customer orientation *n* [U] when a company finds out about its customers' needs, and offers products and services that satisfy these needs

customer relationship management (CRM) *n* [U] a company's activities to keep its customers satisfied, find out more about their needs etc

cyberspace *n* [U] all the sites, services etc on the Internet

debt *n* 1 [C] an amount of money that is owed
2 [U] the state of owing money
3 [U] money borrowed by a company in the form of loans and bonds, rather than shares

decline *v* [I] 1 if an industry or country declines, it becomes less profitable, productive etc
2 if sales, output, production etc decline, they become less – **decline** *n* [C,U]

decrease *v* 1 [I] if an amount, level etc decreases, it goes down
2 [T] if you decrease an amount, level etc, you reduce it – **decrease** *n* [C,U]

delegate *v* [I,T] to give part of your power or work to someone who is at a lower level in the organization – **delegation** *n* [U]

deliver *v* [I,T] 1 to take goods to a place
2 to produce results – **delivery** *n* [C,U]

demand *n* [U] 1 spending on goods and services by companies and people
2 the total amount of a type of goods or services that people or companies buy in a particular period
3 the total amount of a type of goods or services that people or companies would buy if they were available

deputy *n* [C] someone in an organization who is immediately below someone else, and who does their work when they are not there – **deputy** *adj* [only before a noun]

devaluation *n* [C,U] when the value of a country's currency goes down or is reduced by the government, in relation to other currencies

distribute *v* [T] to supply goods to shops, customers etc – **distribution** *n* [U]

distributor *n* [C] a business that makes goods available either to shops or directly to buyers

drive¹ *n* 1 [U] someone's energy, motivation, and ability to work hard
2 [C usually singular] an effort to improve or increase the level of something

drive² *v* [T] 1 to control a train, car etc
2 [usually passive] if an activity is driven by something, it is influenced by it and depends on it

durable *adj* if something is durable, it lasts a long time – **durability** *n* [U]

earnings *n* [plural] 1 the money that a person or particular group of people earn in a particular period
2 the profit made by a company in a particular period, or by

companies in general

economic *adj* 1 [only before a noun] relating to the economy, business etc
2 if an activity is economic, it is profitable

economical *adj* using time, money, goods etc carefully and without wasting any

economically *adv* 1 in a way that relates to the economy, business etc
2 in a way that makes a profit
3 in way that uses time, money, goods etc carefully and without wasting any

economy *n* [C] the system by which a country's goods and services are produced and used, and the people and organizations involved in it

employ *v* [T] to pay someone to work for you in a particular job

employee *n* [C] someone who works for a company, especially in a job below the rank of manager

employee loyalty *n* [U] when employees like working for a particular company, work hard, and do not want to leave

employer *n* [C] a person or organization that employs people

employment *n* [U] 1 work that you do to earn money
2 the number of people in an area, industry etc that have jobs, the type of jobs they have etc

e-tailer *n* [C] a person or organization that sells goods to the public on the Internet

executive *n* [C] someone with an important job as a manager in an organization

expand *v* 1 [I,T] to become larger in size, amount, or number, or to make something larger in size, amount, or number
2 [I] if a company expands, it increases its sales, areas of activity etc – **expansion** *n* [U]

expense *n* 1 [C,U] one of the costs of a particular activity
2 **expenses** [plural] money that an employee spends while they do their job, for example on travel and food, and which their employer then pays back

exploit *v* [T] 1 to treat someone unfairly in order to make money, get an advantage for yourself etc
2 to gain advantage from a situation, opportunity etc

exploitation *n* [U] when you treat someone unfairly in order to make money, get an advantage for yourself etc

export¹ *n* 1 [C usually plural] a product that is sold to another country
2 [U] the sale of products to other countries

export² *v* [I,T] to sell products to other countries

facility *n* 1 [C] a place or large building which is used to make or provide a particular product or service
2 **facilities** [plural] special buildings or equipment that have been provided for a particular use, such as sports activities, shopping, or travelling

failure *n* [C,U] 1 when someone or something does not achieve the results that were expected
2 when a machine stops working

fall¹ *v* *past tense* **fell** *past participle* **fallen** [I] to go down to a lower price, level, amount etc

fall² *n* [C] 1 a reduction in the amount, level, price etc of something
2 when a person or organization loses their position of power or becomes unsuccessful

feature¹ *n* [C] one of the characteristics of a product or service that is useful, attractive etc

feature² *v* [T] if a product features a particular characteristic, it possesses it

finance¹ *n* 1 [U] money that is provided or lent for a particular purpose
2 [U] the department in a company that deals with money
3 **finances** [plural] the situation of a country, company etc in relation to the amount of money it has, owes etc –

financial *adj*

finance[2] *v* [T] to give or lend money for a particular project, activity etc

firm *n* [C] a company

fleet *n* [C] a fleet of cars, trucks etc is all the cars etc that a company owns

flexible *adj* 1 a person, plan etc that is flexible can change or be changed easily to suit any new situation
2 if arrangements for work are flexible, employers can ask workers to do different jobs, work part-time rather than full-time, give them contracts for short periods etc. Flexible working also includes job-sharing and working from home – **flexibility** *n* [U]

flexitime *BrE* **flextime** *AmE n* [U] a system in which people who work in a company do a fixed number of hours each week, but can choose what time they start or finish work within certain limits

focus group *n* [C] a group of people brought together to discuss their feelings and opinions about a particular subject. In market research, focus groups discuss their opinions of products, advertisements, companies etc

forecast[1] *n* [C] a description of what is likely to happen in the future, based on information available now

forecast[2] *v past tense and past participle* **forecast** or **forecasted** [T] to state what is likely to happen in the future, based on information available now

formal *adj* 1 formal behaviour is very polite
2 [only before noun] formal qualifications are those you gain at school, university etc, rather than experience you get in your job

found *v* [T] to start a new activity, organization etc – **founder** *n* [C]

global *adj* 1 affecting or involving the whole world
2 including and considering all the parts of a situation together, rather than the individual parts separately – **globally** *adv*

globalization also **-isation** *BrE n* [U] the tendency for the world economy to work as one unit, led by large international companies doing business all over the world

globalize also **-ise** *BrE v* [I,T] if a company, an industry, or an economy globalizes or is globalized, it no longer depends on conditions in one country, but on conditions in the world as whole

goods *n* [plural] things that are produced in order to be used or sold

gross domestic product (GDP) *n* [singular] the total value of goods and services produced in a country's economy, not including income from abroad

grow *v past tense* **grew** *past participle* **grown** 1 [I] to increase in amount, size, or degree
2 [T] if you grow a business activity, you make it bigger

growth *n* [U] an increase in size, amount, or degree

guarantee *n* [C] a formal written promise to repair or replace a product if there is a fault within a particular period

headquarters *n* [plural] the head office or main building of an organization – **headquartered** *adj*

healthcare *n* [U] medical care, doctors, hospitals etc considered as an industry

high-tech also **hi-tech** *adj* high-tech companies, activities etc use advanced equipment and techniques

hire *v* [T] 1 if a company hires new employees, it recruits them
2 if you hire a car, boat etc you pay to use it for a particular period

human resources *n* [plural] 1 an organization's employees, with their abilities and skills
2 (HR) the administration of a company's employees, including recruitment, salary systems etc

human rights *n* [plural] the basic rights that people have to be treated fairly and equally, especially by their government

image *n* 1 [C] a picture, photograph etc
2 [C,U] all the ideas that people have about a product, person etc, considered together

import[1] *n* [C] a product that is bought from another country

import[2] *v* [I,T] to buy products from other countries

incentive *n* [C] something which is used to encourage people, especially to make them work harder, produce more or spend more money

income *n* [C,U] 1 the amount that a person earns in a particular period
2 the profit made by a company within a particular period

industrial *adj* 1 involving industry, or of a type used in industry
2 industrial areas, countries etc have many different companies and industries

industrialist *n* [C] a powerful businessman or businesswoman

industry *n* 1 [U] the production of basic materials or finished goods
2 [U] all the people and organizations that work in industry
3 [C] a particular type of industry or service

inflation *n* [U] a continuing increase in the price of goods and services, or the rate of this increase

infrastructure *n* [C,U] 1 the basic systems and structures that a country needs to make economic activity possible, for example transport, communications, and power supplies
2 the basic systems and equipment needed for an industry or business to operate successfully or for an activity to happen

innovate *v* [I] to design and develop new and better products – **innovator** *n* [C]

innovation *n* 1 [C] a new idea, method, or invention
2 [U] the introduction of new ideas or methods

innovative *adj* 1 an innovative product, method, process etc is new, different, and better than those that existed before
2 using clever new ideas and methods – **innovatively** *adv*

insurance *n* [U] an arrangement where a company collects money from a person or organization and, in return, promises to pay them money if they are ill, have an accident, cause harm to others etc

interest *n* 1 [U] an amount paid by a borrower to a lender, for example to a bank by someone borrowing money for a loan, or by a bank to someone keeping money in an account there
2 [U] the interest rate at which a particular sum of money is borrowed and lent
3 [C] the part of a company that someone owns
4 [C] the possession of rights, especially to land, property etc

interest rate *n* [C] the cost of borrowing money, expressed as a percentage over a particular period such as a month or year

interpreter *n* [C] someone who translates what someone says from one language into another, especially as their job

inventory *n* [U] the American word for stocks of goods

invest *v* [I,T] 1 to put money into a business activity, hoping to make a profit
2 to buy shares, bonds etc, hoping to make a profit – **investment** *n* [C,U]

invoice *n* [C] a document sent by a supplier to a customer showing how much they owe for particular goods or services

issue *n* [C] 1 something that must be discussed, decided etc
2 a magazine or newspaper appearing on a particular date

join *v* [I,T] if you join a company, you start working for it

joint venture *n* [C] a business activity in which two or more companies have invested together

labor union *n* [C] *AmE* an organization representing people working in a particular industry or profession, especially in meetings with their employers. Labor unions are called trade unions in British English

labour *BrE,* **labor** *AmE n* [U] 1 the work performed by the people in a company, country etc

2 the people doing this work considered as a group

labour force *BrE*, **labor force** *AmE n* [C] another name for workforce

launch[1] *v* [I,T] 1 to show or make a new product available for sale for the first time

2 to start a new company

3 to start a new activity, usually after planning it carefully

launch[2] *n* [C] 1 an occasion at which a new product is shown or made available for sale or use for the first time

2 the start of a new activity or plan

level[1] *n* [C] 1 the measured amount of something that exists at a particular time or in a particular place

2 all the people or jobs within an organization, industry etc that have similar importance and responsibility

level[2] *v* **levelled, levelling** *BrE* **leveled, leveling** *AmE*

level off/out *phr v* [I] to stop climbing or growing and become steady or continue at a fixed level

liability *n* 1 [singular] an amount of money owed by a business to a supplier, lender, or other creditor

2 **liabilities** [plural] the amounts of money owed by a business considered together, as shown in its balance sheet

3 [U] a person's or organization's responsibility for loss, damage, or injury caused to others or their property, or for payment of debts

licensing agreement *n* [C] an arrangement where one company gives permission to another to make products based on its ideas, usually in exchange for payment

lifecycle also **life-cycle** *n* [C] the different stages in the existence of a product, from its design and launch, through to the time when it is discontinued (= no longer sold)

lifestyle *n* [C,U] the way someone lives, including their job, how they spend their money etc

limited company also **limited liability company** *n* [C] a company where individual shareholders lose only the cost of their shares if the company goes bankrupt, and not other property they own

liquidation *n* [U] if a company goes into liquidation, it stops operating and all its remaining assets are sold

loan *n* [C] an amount of money that is lent, usually in return for interest until the money is repaid

logo *n* [C] a design or way of writing its name that a company or organization uses as its official sign on its products, advertising etc

lose *v past tense* and *past participle* **lost** *present participle* **losing** [T] 1 to stop having something any more, or to have less of it

2 to have less money than you had before or to spend more money than you are receiving

3 **lose something (to sb/sth)** to have something such as a contract or customers taken away by someone or something

loss *n* 1 [C,U] the fact of no longer having something that you used to have

2 [C] when a business or part of a business spends more money in costs than it gets in sales in a particular period, or loses money on a particular deal, problem etc

maintenance *n* [U] the work, repairs etc required to keep something in good condition

manage *v* [T] to direct or control an organization or part of one

management *n* [U] 1 the activity or skill of directing or controlling the work of an organization, or part of one

2 the managers of an organization considered together

3 the managers in charge of a particular activity, and the skills and knowledge that they need

manager *n* [C] someone whose job is to manage all or part of an organization

managing director (MD) *n* [C usually singular] in the UK, the manager with the most authority in the day-to-day management of a company. The job of MD is sometimes combined with that of chairperson

manufacture *v* [T] to make goods – **manufacturer** *n* [C] – **manufacturing** *n* [U]

market[1] *n* [C] all the people and organizations involved in the activity of buying and selling particular goods or services

market[2] *v* [T] 1 to sell something or make it available for sale

2 to sell something by considering what customers want, how much they are willing to pay, where they want to buy it etc

marketing *n* [U] activities to design and sell a product or service by considering what customers want, how much they are willing to pay, where they want to buy it etc

marketing mix *n* [C usually singular] the combination of marketing actions often referred to as product, price, place, and promotion: selling the right product, through appropriate distribution channels, and at the right price in relation to other products so that the company makes a profit, with the correct support in terms of advertising etc

market share *n* [C,U] the sales of a particular company in a market, expressed as a percentage of the total sales

mentor *n* [C] an experienced person who gives advice to less experienced people to help them in their work

merchandise *n* [U] goods that are produced in order to be sold, especially goods that are sold in a store

merge *v* [I,T] if two or more companies, organizations etc merge, or if they are merged, they join together

merger *n* [C] an occasion when two or more companies, organizations etc join together to form a larger company etc

model *n* [C] 1 a particular type or design of a vehicle or machine

2 a simple description or structure that is used to help people understand similar systems or structures

morale *n* [U] the level of confidence and positive feelings among a group of people who work together

motivate *v* [T] 1 to encourage someone and make them want to achieve something and be willing to work hard in order to do it

2 to provide the reason why someone does something – **motivated** *adj*

motivation *n* 1 [U] eagerness and willingness to do something without needing to be told or forced to do it

2 [C] the reason why you want to do something

multinational *n* [C] a large company that has offices, factories and business activities in many different countries

net[1] *adj* a net amount of money is the amount that remains after costs, taxes etc have been taken away

net[2] also **Net** *n* [singular] the Internet

network *n* [C] a group of people, organizations, offices etc that work together

niche also **niche market** *n* [C] a market for a product or service, perhaps an expensive or unusual one that does not have many buyers but that may be profitable for companies who sell it

numeracy *n* [U] when people are good at arithmetic and can deal with numbers without difficulty – **numerate** *adj*

online also **on-line** *adj, adv* involving the use of the Internet to obtain and exchange information, buy goods etc

outlet *n* [C] a shop or other organization through which products are sold

overdraft *n* [C] *especially BrE* an arrangement between a bank and a customer allowing them to take out more money from their account than they had in it

overtime *n* [U] 1 time that you spend working in your job in addition to your normal working hours

2 time that a factory, office etc is operating in addition to its normal hours

3 the money that you are paid for working more hours than

usual

overwork *n* [U] when someone works too much or too hard – **overworked** *adj*

parent company *n* [C] a company that owns more than half the shares in another. The other company is its subsidiary

partner *n* [C] 1 a company that works with another company in a particular activity, or invests in the same activity
2 someone who starts a new business with someone else by investing in it
3 a member of certain types of business or professional groups, for example partnerships of lawyers, architects etc

payback period *n* [C] the length of time that it takes to get back the investment put into a particular project, and to start making a profit

payment *n* [C,U] the act of paying money to someone, or the amount involved

payment system *n* [C] the arrangements for paying employees in a particular company including bonuses, overtime etc

pharmaceuticals *n* [plural] medicines, and the industry that produces them – **pharmaceutical** *adj*

phase¹ *n* [C] a particular stage or period in doing something

phase² *v* [T] if you phase something over a period, you do it gradually during that period

pie chart *n* [C] a drawing of a circle divided into several sections, where the size of each section represents an amount as a percentage of the whole

plc abbreviation for public limited company

president *n* [C] in the US, the most important person on the board of directors of a company

private sector *n* [singular] all the companies in a country that are not owned by the government, considered as a whole

privatize also **-ise** *BrE v* [T] if a government privatizes a company that it owns, it sells it to investors – **privatization** *n* [C,U]

promote *v* [I,T] 1 to help something develop and grow
2 to give someone a more important job or rank in an organization
3 to sell a product using advertising, free gifts etc

promotion *n* [C,U] 1 a move to a more important job or rank in a company or organization
2 also **sales promotion** advertisements, free gifts and other activities intended to sell a product or service

public limited company *n* [C] in the UK, a form of limited company whose shares are freely sold and traded. Public limited companies have the letters PLC after their name

public sector *n* [singular] all the companies and business activities owned and controlled by the government of a particular country, considered as a group

purchase *n* [C] the act of buying something, or the thing that you buy – **purchase** *v* [T] – **purchasing** *n* [U]

qualification *n* 1 [C usually plural] an examination that you have passed at school, university, or in your profession
2 [C] a skill, personal quality, or type of experience that makes you suitable for a particular job

R and D *n* [U] research and development; the part of a business concerned with studying new ideas and developing new products

range *n* [C] a set of similar products made by a particular company or sold in a particular shop

rate *n* [C] 1 the speed at which something happens
2 the number of examples of something, often expressed as a percentage
3 another name for interest rate

raw material *n* [C usually plural] one of the basic materials used to make something. For example, steel is one of the raw materials in cars

record¹ *n* 1 [C] the past performance of a person, organization etc
2 **records** [plural] the history of a particular activity, organization etc

record² *adj* [only before a noun] involving the best level, performance etc in a particular activity

recruit¹ *v* [I,T] to find new people to work for an organization, do a job etc

recruit² *n* [C] someone who has recently joined a company or organization

recruitment *n* 1 [U] the process or the business of recruiting new people
2 [C] an occasion when someone is recruited

redundancy *n especially BrE* [C,U] when someone loses their job in a company because the job is no longer needed

redundant *adj especially BrE* if you are redundant or made redundant, your employer no longer has a job for you

refund *n* [C] a sum of money that is given back to you if, for example, you are not satisfied with something you have bought – **refund** *v* [T]

relationship *n* [C] the behaviour and feelings of two or more people, companies etc that work together

reliable *adj* someone or something that is reliable can be trusted or depended on – **reliability** *n* [U]

relocate *v* [I,T] if a company or workers relocate or are relocated, they move to a different place – **relocation** *n* [C,U]

rep *n* [C] an informal name for sales representative

representative *n* [C] 1 someone chosen to speak or make decisions for another person or group of people
2 a sales representative

resign *v* [I,T] to officially leave a job, position etc usually through your own choice, rather than being told to leave – **resignation** *n* [C]

resource *n* 1 [C usually plural] also **natural resource** something such as oil, land, or natural energy that exists in a country and can be used to increase its wealth
2 **resources** [plural] all the money, property, skill, labour etc that a company, country etc has available

restructure *v* [I,T] if someone restructures a company, they change the way it is organized, usually in order to make it more profitable – **restructuring** *n* [U]

results *n* [plural] 1 things that happen because of someone's efforts, work etc
2 the profit or loss made by a company in a particular period

retail *v* [I,T] to sell goods to the general public in shops etc – **retailing** *n* [U]

retailer *n* [C] 1 a business that sells goods to members of the public
2 a person or company that owns or runs a shop or chain of shops selling goods to the public

retail outlet *n* [C] a shop through which products are sold to the public

retain *v* [T] if a company retains its customers or employees, they continue to buy from or work for the company, and do not go elsewhere – **retention** *n* [U]

revenue *n* [U] also **revenues** [plural] the amount a company receives from sales in a particular period

rights *n* [plural] 1 the freedom and advantages that everyone should be allowed to have – see also **human rights**
2 if a person or company has the rights to something, they are legally allowed to use it to make money

rise¹ *v past tense* **rose** *past participle* **risen** [I] to increase in number, amount, or value

rise² *n* 1 [C] an increase in number, amount, or value
2 [C] also **pay rise** *BrE* an increase in salary or wages. A rise is called a raise or pay raise in American English
3 [singular] the process of becoming more important, successful, or powerful

sack *v* **give sb the sack/get the sack** to tell someone to leave their job, or to be told to leave your job

sale *n* 1 [C] the act of selling something
2 **for sale** available to be bought
3 **sales** [plural] goods sold in a particular period, or the amount of money received from this

sales representative also **sales rep** *n* [C] someone whose job is to sell their company's products or services, for example by visiting customers

schedule *n* [C] a plan or timetable for doing something

scheduled flight *n* [C] a normal flight on an airline available for anyone to use

sector *n* [C] a particular industry or activity or group of industries etc

secure *adj* involving actions to keep someone or something safe from being damaged, stolen etc – **security** *n* [U]

segment *n* [C] 1 a part of the economy of a country or a company's work
2 also **market segment** a group of customers that share similar characteristics, such as age, income, interests, social class etc
3 also **market segment** the products in a particular part of the market

share *n* [C] 1 one of the parts into which ownership of a company is divided
2 also **market share** the sales of a particular company in a market, expressed as a percentage of the total sales

shareholder *n* [C] a person or organization that owns shares in a company

shareholder value *n* [U] the idea that companies should produce the best possible profit for their shareholders, and that one of the main jobs of management is to ensure this

ship *v* [T] to transport and deliver goods

skill *n* [C,U] an ability to do something well, especially because you have learned and practised it – **skilled** *adj*

slogan *n* [C] an easily remembered phrase used to express a particular idea, for example in an advertisement

smart *adj* 1 intelligent
2 attractive
3 well-dressed
4 relating to technology that does things in an efficient way

sponsorship *n* [U] financial support given to an arts or sports event in order to get public attention

spreadsheet *n* [C] a computer program that shows rows and columns of figures, and allows calculations to be done on them. Spreadsheets are used to analyze what would happen in different situations, for example to sales and profits

stable *adj* firm, steady, or unchanging

start-up *n* [C] a new company, especially a hi-tech one

status *n* [U] 1 your social or professional rank or position
2 high social position that makes people respect you

stereotype *n* [C] a fixed idea about something, that may or may not be true

stock *n* [C,U] 1 *especially AmE* one of the shares into which ownership of a company is divided, or these shares considered together
2 also **stocks** [plural] a supply of a commodity (= oil, metal, farm product etc) that has been produced and is kept to be used when needed
3 *especially BrE* a supply of raw materials or parts before they are used in production, or a supply of finished goods. Stocks of raw materials or parts are usually called inventories in American English
4 a supply of goods, kept for sale by a shop or other retailer. Stocks of goods are usually called inventories in American English

stock market also **stockmarket** *n* [C] a place or computer system where bonds, shares etc are bought and sold

strategy *n* 1 [C] a plan or series of plans for achieving an aim, especially relating to the best way for an organization to develop
2 [U] the process of skilful planning in general

strength *n* [C,U] a particular quality or ability that gives someone an advantage in relation to others

stress *n* [U] continuous feelings of worry about your work or personal life, that prevent you from relaxing – **stressful** *adj*

stressed also **stressed out** *adj* if someone is stressed or stressed out, they are so worried and tired that they cannot relax

subsidiary also **subsidiary company** *n* [C] a company that is at least half-owned by another company, its parent company

subsidize also **-ise** *BrE v* [T] if a government or organization subsidizes a company, activity etc, it pays part of the cost – **subsidized** *adj*

subsidy *n* [C] money that is paid by a government or organization to make something cheaper to buy, use, or produce

supply *v* [T] to sell and provide goods or services – **supplier** *n* [C]

survey *n* [C] 1 a set of questions given to a group of people to find out their opinions
2 the information obtained by analyzing the answers to these questions

tactic *n* [C usually plural] a method that you use to achieve something

takeover *n* [C] an occasion when a person or company obtains control of another company by buying more than half of its shares

talent *n* [C,U] a natural skill or ability

target[1] *n* [C] 1 an organization, industry, country etc that is deliberately chosen to have something done to it
2 a result such as a total, an amount, or a time which you aim to achieve

target[2] *v* [T] 1 to make something have an effect on a particular limited group or area
2 to choose someone or something as your target – **targeted** *adj*

tend *v* [I] if something tends to happen, it happens frequently, but not always

tendency *n* [C] 1 if you have a tendency to do something, you do it frequently
2 the general way in which a particular situation is changing or developing

trade[1] *n* 1 [U] buying and selling goods and services, especially between countries – see also **balance of trade**
2 [C] a particular business activity

trade[2] *v* [I,T] 1 to buy and sell goods and services, especially between countries
2 to buy and sell shares etc on a financial market

trademark also **trade-mark** *n* [C] a name, sign, or design on a product to show that it is made by a particular company

trade union *n* [C] *BrE* an organization representing people working in a particular industry or profession, especially in meetings with their employers. Trade unions are called labor unions in American English

trading group *n* [C] a group of countries that agree to have low or no taxes on goods they export to each other

transaction *n* [C] 1 a business deal, especially one involving the exchange of money
2 the act of paying or receiving money

transfer *v* [I,T usually passive] if you transfer to another job or workplace, or if you are transferred, you move there

trend *n* [C] the general way in which a particular situation is changing or developing

turnover *n* [singular] 1 *BrE* the amount of business done in a particular period, measured by the amount of money obtained from customers for goods or services that have been sold

2 the rate at which workers leave an organization and are replaced by others

3 the rate at which goods are sold and stock is replaced

unemployed *adj* without a job

unemployment *n* [U] 1 when you do not have a job

2 also **unemployment rate** the number of people in a particular area, country etc who do not have a job

union *n* [C] 1 a group of people, countries etc who work together for a particular aim

2 a trade union or labor union

unskilled *adj* without training in the skills needed in particular jobs

update *n* [C] information that tells you what has happened recently in a particular activity, situation etc

vacancy *n* [C] a job that is available

virtual *adj* involving something that gives you the experience of its real equivalent

visual also **visual aid** *n* [C] a diagram, map etc that people can look at, for example in a presentation, and that helps them understand and remember it

voice mail also **voicemail** *n* [U] a system for leaving messages for people by telephone, or the messages themselves

volunteer *v* [I] to ask to do something that you do not have to do – **volunteer** *n* [C]

warehouse *n* [C] a building where goods are stored

weakness *n* [C,U] lack of a particular characteristic that would give you the ability to succeed, perform better etc

website *n* [C] information about a particular company, subject etc available on the Internet. Each website has an address that begins 'http'

wholesaler *n* [C] a person or company that sells goods in large quantities to other wholesalers, or to retailers who may then sell them to the general public

workaholic *n* [C] someone who cannot stop work and is unwilling to do anything else

workforce *n* [C] all the people who work in a particular country, area, industry, company, or place of work

workload *n* [C] the work that a person or group of people have to do in a particular period